BEGOTTEN
with Love

EVERY FAMILY HAS ITS STORY

Jo Ann V. Glim

BEGOTTEN: With Love

BEGOTTEN
with Love

EVERY FAMILY HAS ITS STORY

Jo Ann V. Glim

BEGOTTEN: With Love
– *Every Family Has Its Story* 2nd Edition
Copyright © 2013 by Jo Ann V. Glim. All rights reserved.

No part of this publication may be reproduced, stored in a retrieval system, or transmitted in any way by any means, electronic, mechanical, photocopy, recording, or otherwise, without the prior written permission of the copyright holder, except as provided by USA copyright law.

Despite the author's desire to relate the historical portion of the story as accurately as possible, there is no way to say with absolute certainty that all the information within this book is historically correct. The author and publisher are not responsible for any inaccuracies within the manuscript.

Published by: Stemma Books, LLC.
P.O. Box 174, Bradenton, FL 34206
JGlim@tampabay.rr.com
www.BEGOTTENtheBook.com

ISBN: 978-0-9888129-1-0 (pbk.)

ISBN: 978-0-9888129-1-8 (pbk.) 2nd Edition – Includes Forward

ISBN: 978-0-9888129-2-5 (ebk.)

LCN: TX 7-720-177

Category: History / American History / Biography / Creative Non-Fiction / Debut Author

Edited by: Erin Roof

Book Cover Design and Digital Formatting / Layout by:
Eli Blyden | www.CrunchTimeGraphics.com

Printed in the United States of America

Dedicated To:

My Beloved Husband, Bill

Tammy and Laura

John, Jace, and Melisa

and Generations to Come

BEGOTTEN: With Love

Preface

This book is a glimpse into family life, generations past and present. Our ancestors came to America with a vision of a better future, free of tyranny and repression for descendants to come.

They were patriots and inventors, dreamers and doers. They recognized that freedom came with a price . . . sometimes the ultimate price. They were courageous and self-sacrificing, independent and hardworking. They lived according to Christian morals, values, and principles. They believed in honesty and respect and understood choices have consequences and rewards. Some achieved wealth beyond imaginings. Others lived as paupers. Most enjoyed good health, while a few persevered through physical misfortune.

Throughout the generations heroes and heroines, cowards and cads brought dreams for a better tomorrow. Their visions and tenacity helped form our great country and mold the dynamics of the American family. They struggled, doubted, and questioned, but they persevered with discipline, faith, and respect. They celebrated personal victories, consoled each other in times of trouble, and believed in optimism and hope.

For those of us whose time is now, our unscripted chapters will be added to the annals of family history, tested and defined by those surrounding us. Their opinions will be influenced by society and world history and the core values *they* hold dear. Only the individual knows the true temperament he or she possesses and the values with which they live. In the end, no one opinion defines who we are, and the *only* relationship that matters is the one we have with God Almighty. With that being said, it serves us all well to remember that how we conduct ourselves can be measured by the adage: "adversity does not build character, it reveals it."

Be mindful of who you are. Choose wisely. Live kindly and courageously. Love deeply. Use your talents for the good of the family, our country, and others. Give all glory to God because nothing in life is possible without Him.

Families are an ever-evolving chain of events filled with characters and shared genetics. We are all flawed. We are all beautiful. We are all one in an essential Master plan.

Knowledge expands understanding;

Understanding increases awareness;

Awareness reveals compassion;

Compassion seeks truth;

Truth begs for action;

Action relies on knowledge.

Contents

Dedicated To: v

Preface vii

Foreword xv

Author's Note... xvi

Introduction.. xvii

SCOTCH / IRISH / ENGLISH CONNECTION
PATERNAL HISTORY

PART I: The Paternal History (1864-1936) introduces readers to a family strong of will, courageous in spirit and flawed by alcohol. Geographically, this part of the story is set in Scotland, South Carolina, Georgia, Alabama, Colorado and California.

Chapter 1   1864   Nothing Civil About War............................ 1
Sannie nears death as Cameron fights Sherman's troops

Chapter 2   1874   The Visit... 9
Meddling has its consequences

Chapter 3   1884   Cheers and Tears...................................... 15
Adam swears allegiance to America

Chapter 4   1902   Mile High Dreams..................................... 31
Adam's health crisis seals the family's fate

Chapter 5   1916   Prophecy 37
    Archie is forewarned

Chapter 6   1924   Promises… Promises 43
    It's high stakes wrestling with the Devil

Chapter 7   1924   Innocence Lost 53
    Tragedy steals Tom's innocence

Chapter 8   1934   A Hand Up 65
    Tom joins the CCC

Chapter 9   1935   Love, Honor and Obey 77
    Edith trusts a stranger

Chapter 10 1936   Coast to Coast 83
    Spike recovers from stabbing while Archie regrets the past

SWEDISH CONNECTION
MATERNAL HISTORY

PART II: The Maternal History (1892-1929) allows readers to meet a family of visionaries. Sven described himself to the immigration board at Ellis Island as an experimental engineer. He and his brother, John, held many patents for their various inventions. John more sensibly referred to himself as a design engineer. Although no one remembers his name, John Andersson Arton invented the mechanism necessary to operate the hide-a-bed we all enjoy in our homes today.

Chapter 11   1892   Amerika 93
  John survives the high seas

Chapter 12   1896   Indentured Servitude 101
  Hedvig pays a price for freedom

Chapter 13   1896   Dare to Dream 111
  The wheels of progress are defined

Chapter 14   1902   Sparks Fly 119
  John overcomes his fear of commitment

Chapter 15   1904   The Parcel 125
  The newlyweds receive unexpected news

Chapter 16   1920   Patience Pays 129
  A new chair design brings John celebrity status

Chapter 17   1923   Hidden Treasure 135
  The Raven holds the key

Chapter 18   1926   Vikings' Valhalla 141
  John and Hedvig prepare for Heaven

Chapter 19   1929   Sugar Bowl Economics 147
        Depression rocks the home

SWEDISH / SCOTCH / IRISH / ENGLISH
BLENDED HISTORY

PART III: The Blended History (1942-1957) reveals the dreams, challenges and talents of the two family units as they evolve in a world besieged by post-Depression and World War II events. This new generation is bonded in war-time/whirlwind love yet divided by societal pressures. Personal choices set the course for future generations.

Chapter 20   1942   Love and War 153
        Tom trains for WW II, Verna volunteers at USO

Chapter 21   1942   Romance and Roller Coasters 159
        Tom and Verna take the plunge

Chapter 22   1947   Sea Stories 165
        Buddies, Beer and Bull

Chapter 23   1948   Atonement 169
        Nothing good comes from two wrongs

Chapter 24   1948   Keeping Peace 173
        When emotion and intellect collide, choices clash

Chapter 25   1948   Family Matters 179
        Keeping bonds strong means sacrifice

Chapter 26   1949   God Jul 183
        Celebrating the Old Fashioned way

Chapter 27   1951   Across the Miles 187
        Joanie tells the truth, Tom drops a bombshell

Chapter 28   1952   Family Lore 193
        History passed on through stories

Chapter 29   1954   Rite to Work 199
          Menial labor has its rewards

Chapter 30   1957   Ecclesiastes 3 205
          Life in small town America, John catches an intruder

SWEDISH / SCOTCH / IRISH / ENGLISH
FUTURE HISTORY

PART IV: Those in the **Future History (1958-2003)** segment face the transitions of generations but not in the order expected. Pummeled by disappointments and death, the family accepts lessons in patience and forgiveness and in turn finds internal happiness and peace.

Chapter 31   1958   Forever Changing 215
          Joanie struggles with the angst of maturing

Chapter 32   1958   Bodings 219
          The family ignores warning signs

Chapter 33   1958   Collateral Offenses 225
          Deeds carry consequences

Chapter 34   1958   Out of Order 229
          Joanie copes with death

Chapter 35   1959   Best Laid Plans 235
          John fends off attack

Chapter 36   1961   Night Visitors 243
          FBI interrogates the neighborhood

Chapter 37   2003   At Looooong Last 249
          Finding peace

Acknowledgements 257
Bibliography 259
Author's Biography 265

Foreword

By: Carolyn Tolentino

Some years ago, Joanie conveyed her intentions of sharing the remarkable stories of her ancestors with her daughters and grandchildren. The book was to be *just* for them, but after hearing vignettes of her story over the phone, I was impressed with her descriptive and moving style. Many of us closest to Joanie encouraged her to publish the memoirs for the public, since the messages of love, faith, hope, courage, and forgiveness are for anyone who has been part of a family.

The author and I have been best friends for sixty-five years! Joanie was four years old and I five when we first met. Not long after becoming acquainted, we vowed to be blood sisters forever. We were inseparable. Either we were searching for tadpoles in a nearby creek, picking blackberries on vacant lots and selling them door to door, playing at each other's homes, or exploring our hometown on our bikes. During the 1940s and '50s, no one worried when or where children roamed in the neighborhoods of Anacortes.

BEGOTTEN: With Love gives a keen and loving portrait of this family in their younger days. As a child, I never gave a thought to anyone's parents or grandparents as being young or vital, my own included.

However, this glimpse into the past has prompted me, and may prompt you, to discover the journey our ancestors experienced. This book has given me the motivation to complete a grandparent's journal my son and his wife bought for me when my grandson was born. Apart from inspiring interest in one's own ancestral history, *BEGOTTEN: With Love* is just a heartwarming and uplifting read.

Author's Note

The family portrayed is real. The stories are true, with few stretches of the imagination. Most supporting characters are fictionalized yet based on recollections and/or incidents retold throughout the years. Historical events, people, and dates of importance have been verified and documented.

The Following Pages Contain:

LEGENDS & LORE / LESSONS / LEGACY

(not necessarily in that order)

Introduction

I thought the best way to introduce this story to you is to relate how it began for me in 1979.

Aunt Frances, a petite Italian woman, looked even tinier sitting on the upholstered rocking chair in her bedroom with a massive Bible dwarfing her lap. She was still wearing her mourning dress.

"Uncle Spike wanted you to have this after he died, Joanie. It belonged to your grandmother and contains the family's history . . . at least part of it. He told me it's up to you to find the rest."

She caressed the ornate detailing on the leather-bound cover for a moment before she looked at her thirty-five-year-old niece and said, "By the way, your maiden name is not Elliott."

That was the beginning of this odyssey.

Scotch / Irish / English Connection

CHAPTER 1

1864

Nothing Civil about War

The young girl's body barely made a lump in the bed upon which she laid. Her long, dark hair was lovingly twisted into a braid by her mother. Still, run-away tresses soaked with sweat clung to her cheeks.

"Mama?" Sannie cried out with terror. "Mama the bummers—they're on the ridge. See them? Do you see them?"

Her legs began to move. She opened her mouth to scream. Her mother cradled the child's feverish head and gently laid it back on the bed.

"How long's she been like that?" asked the man standing in the shadows.

"At least five days," said the young woman as she dampened the child's face with a cool, wet rag.

"Damn them. Damn them to hell!"

Cameron poked at the last remnants of wood in the fireplace. A low grunt accompanied every jab. "All our food . . . gone. The livestock, what they couldn't carry off, slaughtered. The barn burnt to the ground. How are we to live? What kind of monsters are these men, Maggie? For God's sake—winter's coming. We've got a sick child that might not live."

"Don't say that, Cameron," Maggie pleaded with tears streaming down her face.

"Look at her!" Cameron said, swinging around and pointing at the tiny body.

Sannie saw the ember glow on the end of the poker. "No! No! You stay away! Daddy will take care of you!" Sannie screamed in her delirium.

"Dorinda!" she cried out. There was no answer. "Where's my sister, Mama?"

"She's sleeping," said Maggie. "I want you to do the same. Now hush child."

Her mother began to softly sing, "Tura lura lura, Tura lura lie / Tura lura lura, it's an Irish lull-a-by."

Cameron was captured by his wife's beauty. You could see she was exhausted from caring for Sannie and fending off the foraging soldiers, but her fine, white skin and soft blue-gray eyes spoke of the genteel, Southern spirit within.

"For God's sake, Maggie, she's right! It is up to her daddy to take care of them," he said.

He sank back onto the wooden rocking chair next to the hearth and spotted a musket ball wedged in the ceiling from the skirmish in their side yard yesterday. The volley of gunfire ripped a shutter from its hinges, and glass from the windowpane shattered upon the floor next to the child's bed. After the battle, Maggie swept up the shards while he placed chinking in the holes. *This beautiful plantation . . .* he thought bitterly. *Gone is the kitchen, the hen house, the smoke house, the slave quarters. The darkies run off. Everything we've worked for . . . gone.*

He looked at the window and muttered under his breath, "All we have left is a handful of hay and a whole lot of cow shit."

He hung his head and clenched his teeth, fighting back his anger. Maggie's garden, her pride and joy, had been trampled by the horses. Blood spattered on the trough. Yankee blood. Confederate blood.

"Bobby Ray took a bayonet to the side, you know," Cameron said. "His wife says he's not doing well."

"I know," Maggie whispered as she rubbed her husband's shoulders.

"Old Man McCaffery was hung by his balls in the barn until he told them where he hid Miss Ruby's jewelry. And then they killed him. They killed him! A seventy-six-year-old man. Damn them!"

Cameron got up and walked to his daughter's bedside. "How long she had that rash, Maggie?"

"It started this afternoon."

"She's got the pox, you know," he said quietly. "She may die."

Maggie buried her head into her apron and sobbed. "She's only seven years old."

Cameron grabbed his musket and beaver coat and headed for the door.

"Where are you going?" she asked.

"I think Miss Ida still has a quarantine flag from last summer when her boy had the pox. It'll save me a trip to Doc Porter's," he lied.

"Those soldiers are still lurking about, aren't they," Maggie asked through pressed lips.

She suspected that Cameron and some of the other men (neighbors and townsfolk) patrolled the perimeter of their township not far from Columbus, Georgia. The only men left to protect the homes, women, and children were the elderly, the disabled, and those whose careers made them invaluable to the cause, such as metalsmiths and farmers.

"I'm not leaving you alone any longer than I have to," he said as he stood behind her and wrapped his arms around her waist. His hands rested gently on her growing belly.

He nuzzled her neck and whispered in her ear, "Try and get some rest. I love you, you know."

Morning broke, and the faint rays of pale sunlight promised a fair day. The exhausted child slept. The tiny red marks of yesterday were now lesions filled with fluid on her face, hands, and torso.

Maggie shivered as she drew water from the well. The days were getting shorter, and it wouldn't be long before they'd see their first frost. She looked around the property, wistfully hoping to see her husband coming home, but she knew it was too soon. On foot, it was a day's journey to the edge of their property. She also hoped against all hope that there were no bummers from Sherman's Army lurking in the nearby woods.

The one saving grace for the family was their bunker, a ten-by-ten-foot dirt room dug into the ground and covered with wood and earth. They stored provisions there in case cannon balls were lobbed their way. The trap door, concealed by her prized rose bushes, hid the meager rations that must now carry them through the winter.

Maggie paused for a moment and looked at her home, her beautiful home with the antebellum porches and towering Greek columns . . . scarred by artillery fire. This was a modest plantation by baron standards, but it was enough to support the family and care for their forty-two negroes.

The government passed the Twenty Slave Law a couple of years back, which forced her husband to work their land even though Congress passed laws limiting the amount he sold. Production was down 60 percent and fertile land sat fallow, except for fields planted for personal use.

Now that the South had seceded, cotton and corn crops grew in open fields, the produce used to support the Confederate cause. For months, rumors and news reports from Savannah warned of Sherman's possible March to the Sea. Families prepared as best they could by sending valuables to friends or relatives, storing them out of harm's way. Some buried heirlooms on their property or in the swamps. Others trusted their staff to find a safe haven. Coins were carefully sewn into the hems of women's dresses to be used in an emergency as the confederate dollar lost its value.

Maggie had thirty silver dollars saved for Doc Porter to pay for his services and those of a midwife. Her baby was due in January; only a few more months of confinement and another child would be born. *Dear God, let it be healthy!* was her daily prayer.

Since the raid a couple of days ago, all Maggie could see to the horizon was scorched earth and smoldering fires where plantations, factories, and mills once stood. There was nothing left.

Today's my twenty-eighth birthday, she thought. *It's a far cry from my party three years ago when war was a whisper on the lips of the men.* Names like Brown (the abolitionist) from Kansas, President Lincoln, and his opponent Douglas spiced the smoking parlor's conversations, depending on political persuasion.

Demure smiles from girls in long-flowing skirts belied the pain from being trussed into corsets, let alone worry about loved ones and what the future might hold. Their giggles gilded the halls with tempered joy. Music from the piano filled the home, and children played tag in the side yard with not a care in the world.

Maggie wondered what the conversations would be like at her party if it were held today with the most prominent names of

Stonewall Jackson, General Lee, Ulysses S. Grant, Sherman, and Wilson on the lips of revelers.

She looked at the dust and dirt that streaked her skirt and shoes now. Her nails were cracked and broken. Still, she took a few steps forward and back, reliving a dance in the ballroom.

"Pssst, Miss Maggie!"

Maggie gasped with fright and twirled around.

"It's me and Adisa, Miss Maggie."

"Birtha? Is that you?" Maggie asked in disbelief as she squinted in the direction of the voice. She barely saw the pudgy black fingers clutching the lattice under the side porch.

"What are you doing there?"

"We no place to go, Miss Maggie. We thought they gonna kill us! We ran. We free now but where . . . where we go?"

"How long have you been there, girl?" Maggie asked.

"Two day now."

Birtha couldn't help but stare at the jars of peaches folded in Miss Maggie's apron. Maggie caught her glance and handed her one of the jars.

"Here, you take this. I can't let you in the house. Sannie has smallpox."

"Don't you pay no mind, Miss Maggie. We hep you care for that sweet child just like alway."

Birtha crawled out from under the porch, followed by her grandson, a tall, lanky boy about nineteen years old. The woman's quick steps led her to the side door. She took a long look beyond the smoldering corncrib to the valley below, stared at the wisps of smoke from the enemy camps, let out a deep sigh, and said, "It ain't *never* gonna be the same, Miss Maggie."

"Miss Maggie have hersef a fine baby boy," Birtha said as she dressed the newborn in swaddling.

"That she does," Doc Porter said as he packed up his instruments. He stopped long enough to read the front-page article in the crumpled paper lying on the table. His face turned to stone as he fought back his tears.

THE BLUE AND THE GRAY

News Source of the Confederate – January 1864

CAMERON'S RAIDERS VASTLY OVERPOWERED

The rebels fought courageously against Sherman's marauding infantry through wood and swamp north and east of Atlanta last Friday. All afternoon, Federal carbineers from Wilson's Marauders discharged volleys into their midst. Exhausted, the ragtag band of raiders continued their assault until Union horsemen outflanked them and Cameron, their leader, slumped to the ground mortally wounded.

"He was a good man, Birtha. You tell his son . . . his daddy was a good man."

BEGOTTEN: With Love

CHAPTER 2

1874

The Visit

Sannie's younger sister, Leonora, peered through the parlor's laced curtains as James tethered his horse to the hitching post near the road. When he turned toward the house, she quickly hid behind the heavier woolen drapes and frantically whispered, "Hurry, Sannie, he's almost here!"

Seventeen-year-old Sannie's hands trembled as she carefully filled the sparking lamp and returned it to the wall next to the front door. This tiny, two-inch lantern, designed to protect a single woman's reputation from the wiles of an amorous suitor, limited visits to fifteen minutes . . . unless a resourceful sister pushed the limit by overfilling the oil.

"Don't worry, Miss Leonora," Sannie assured her fifteen-year-old sister. She placed the matches on the foyer table. "Everything's in place."

"Did you overfill it?" Leonora asked in a loud whisper.

"You have enough oil for a twenty-minute visit," Sannie replied confidently.

Both girls jumped at the rap on the door.

"Calm yourself, honey!" Sannie giggled. "You don't want him to see you all dewy!"

"Massa James here for Miss Leonora," Birtha announced as she stood in the parlor doorway.

James stood in the foyer with his hat in hand.

"Ms. Leonora will receive you now," Birtha said and lit the tiny lamp. She shook her finger at the girls and tried to hide a smile as she looked at the level of oil. "Will you be needin' anything more, Miss Leonora?"

"That will be all," the young girl responded.

The three adolescents listened intently as the old woman mumbled under her breath loud enough for James to hear, "Too many long visits from gentlemen callers and tongues gonna wag!" Birtha's heels clicked on the pine planking in the hallway, and a creak of floorboards near the entrance to the sitting room announced to the young adults they were alone.

"Good afternoon, Ms. Leonora," James said. His slicked-down hair accentuated the largeness of his forehead and ears. Leonora giggled and blushed.

"James, would you like to see Mama's rose garden?" Sannie coaxed as she led her shy sister and the gangly suitor toward the door.

The last blush of summer blooms comes late in the south. Maggie tended this garden with extra care. These roses had been her pride at the plantation before it was destroyed. They were the only thing of beauty she had been able to save and bring with to their new home in Prattville, Alabama. These roses were a sweet reminder that life continues.

"I'll set some iced tea on the front porch for you while you're gone."

The Visit

"Thank you, Miss Sannie," James said as he held the door open for Leonora. Her taffeta skirt softly rustled as she brushed past her new beau.

Sannie went to the kitchen, where her mother busily prepared treats for the love-struck couple.

"There's a plate of sugar cookies next to the tea," Maggie said as she balanced her baby on her hip. Sannie took a cookie from under the covered tray.

"Thank you, Mama," she said as she brushed a kiss on her mother's cheek.

Sannie had become very close and protective of her younger sisters and brothers since the war. She felt it her duty to care for them even though Middleton, Sannie's adopted father, and Maggie encouraged her to *socialize . . . enjoy her youth.* She couldn't imagine anyone being attracted to her. Even with a slender four-foot-eleven figure, naturally curly black hair, and lavender eyes, who would want a woman with pox marks on her face? Especially with so many fair ladies in town!

She set the refreshments on the wicker table between the two matching chairs. The main portion of the wraparound porch faced Wetumpka Street. Neighbors strolling on warm summer evenings gathered on the Fisher porch for tea and company before the journey home. It became a daily ritual the family enjoyed. But socializing on a Saturday afternoon was for the young women of the house.

Sannie noticed the front door to the house across the street stood wide open. New neighbors were moving in. Three brothers from Scotland was the rumor.

"Fine young men," Maggie told the neighbors gathered on the porch last evening.

"They'll be working for me at the foundry beginning Monday," Middleton added.

But today was Saturday . . . a balmy, Indian summer day. The scent of burning leaves drifted through the air. A reminder that winter was approaching. A burst of wind loosened a bounty of color from the oak trees lining the dirt road where James's horse was tethered. Shadow Dancer let out a snort as debris blew past his withers. The gelding side-stepped to the end of the hitching post as the dust settled around his hooves.

Sannie laughed at the animal's antics and wandered toward the road, hoping to get a closer look at the new neighbors as she calmed the skittish gelding. Silhouettes passed before the windows of the home across the street, but no one came to the door to claim any of the boxes haphazardly piled on the porch.

The young horse impatiently pawed the ground, knowing Sannie's pocket contained treats. He nudged her back hard enough to push her forward just as Sannie's youngest sister skipped towards them.

"What are you up to?" Pauline asked. "No good, I'll bet!" A mischievous glint in the eye of the five year old warned Sannie that her plan was about to be foiled. Pauline had a talent for spilling the beans!

Sannie bent at the waist—hands on hips, nose to nose, eye to eye with her sibling—and said, "You snitch . . . and you'll wish you hadn't!"

Pauline's chin began to quiver. Her nostrils flared and her lungs slowly filled with air. When upset, that teensy-tiny body could squeal longer and louder than Mr. Poulton's prized hog.

"Oh, mercy. Here it comes," Sannie muttered under her breath as she rolled her eyes and covered her ears. "I'm sorry, Miss

Pauline," Sannie called out as she chased the child down the path toward the house.

"Mama!" Pauline screamed while tears streamed down her face. Her flying feet kept her an arm's length ahead of her older sister.

"You can wear my new hair ribbons," Sannie pleaded as she began to untwist her braid. "See?" she yelled as she held her hand out. It was too late.

Pauline's little feet stomped up the front steps of the house as she screamed, "Mama!"

The door slammed behind her.

Leonora and James came running from the garden. "What was all that fuss?" Leonora asked, out of breath.

"Oh, I just don't know when to hush!" Sannie said as she paced from the porch to the hitching post and back again, holding her head in her hands.

The squeak of the screen door made the three stop motionless. Maggie stood, wiping her hands on a dish towel with the baby snuggled in the crook of her arm. Pauline clung to her mama's skirt. Tear stains streaked the dirt on her flushed cheeks as a smug smile crossed her face.

"Change of plans," Sannie said as she pulled the back hem of her skirt through her legs and tied the ends around her waist. Her black, cotton stockings showed all the way to her knees!

Leonora spun James around so he couldn't see her sister's crass behavior.

In one fluid motion, Sannie mounted the horse. A quick jab to the flank and they were off at a full gallop down Wetumpka street on their way to . . . where? Who knew! Why? Who cared!

Adam and his older brother, Daniel, were drawn to the porch of their new home by the commotion heard in the street.

Archie, the youngest of the three Weir brothers, sat on the window ledge, watching the loose road dirt spin into a dust cloud behind the hooves of the racing horse.

"That was quite a little sort out," he said to his brothers in a rolling brogue, his sides shaking with laughter. Then Archie grinned and said, "I think we're going to like this neighborhood."

CHAPTER 3

1884

Cheers and Tears

"Good morning," Sannie sleepily whispered to her husband as she kissed him awake.

"What time is it?" he asked as he rolled over and pulled her into him.

"It's still early. The kids aren't even up."

Adam laughed and nodded towards the end of the bed. Three sets of eyes looked back.

"Come here, my little sweethearts," Sannie beckoned.

The children clambered onto the mattress and under the goose down quilt. Archie was their firstborn and mature for eight. He was much too old to jump on the bed with the little ones.

"Papa," he said, coming no closer than the door, "Uncle Eddie's out front. We're going to polish the tack for Liberty and Freedom," he said and disappeared down the stairs.

"He's a fine lad, Sannie." Adam beamed.

The boy had the black, wavy hair of his mother and the flashing blue-gray eyes of his father. His square jaw and proud walk reminded Adam of his father in Scotland. Ah, Scotland, the place of his birth, homeland of his ancestors. His sister and father still lived a half-day's walk from Glasgow.

"Is anybody else hungry?" Adam asked as he lifted the children off the bed and gently placed them on the floor. "Who wants bacon and eggs for breakfast?"

"Yeah!" The kids squealed and ran to the kitchen.

Sannie heard shouts of "I want hotcakes!" and buried her head under the pillow; morning sickness was just one swallow from reality.

"Are you okay?" Adam asked.

"I'll be right there," was the muffled reply.

Alone in the bedroom, Sannie looked at Adam's suit hanging on the peg on the wall. She smiled with pride as she realized what a special day this was.

"Don't drop the eggs, Philip!" she heard Adam yell right before the splat.

Formal picture of the Weir brothers (l–r): Archie, Adam, Daniel

The humidity was already beginning to rise this morning, but the soft breeze blowing up the street off the creek kept the heat at bay. Adam and Sannie waited for Daniel and Mary Ellen in front of the two-story courthouse on Factory Road across the creek from Pratt's Manufactory.

"Is my tie straight?" Adam asked his wife while mindlessly polishing his shoe tops on the back of his trouser legs.

"You look wonderful," she said as she repositioned the wayward points on his bow tie.

Adam fidgeted with his watch fob and thought of everything that led up to this day. How indebted he was to three men in particular: his father, willing to sacrifice his personal dream for that of his sons; Daniel Pratt, founder of Prattville, Alabama, and the Cotton Gin Mill; and Middleton Fisher, the foundry's manager and Adam's father-in-law. This day was nine years in the making.

"Had a bit of a lay-in this mornin' did ya?" Adam shouted at his brother, Daniel.

Daniel looked to the heavens and shook his head. He was tying up the dray team as kids tumbled off the platform buggy, his three and Adam's four. He pulled at the collar of his suit and stretched his neck, looking for a little wiggle room.

"Whooooa, Dixie," Archie, the youngest of the three brothers, commanded his quarter horse as he drew up to the hitching post. He dismounted and pulled at his trousers as he hurried towards the family. Neither Adam nor his brothers were accustomed to wearing the three-piece Ditto suits with matching waistcoats. They were forge men, used to a working man's attire and the smell of sweat and heat from the foundry on the banks of Autauga creek.

Twelve years ago (Daniel, twenty-four, Adam, nineteen, and Archie, fifteen) worked alongside their father at the sugar mill in Glasgow, Scotland, as apprentices at the forge. The port town bustled with action. Its reputation as a textile leader in Europe drew merchants and buyers from all over the world.

"I've something to show ye," their father said on that evening so long ago.

A yellowed newspaper clipping dropped to the floor from a small chest on the table next to his chair.

Archie Weir, Sr.

PRATTVILLE:
THE WORLDWIDE LEADER OF COTTON GINS
read the headline. The boys listened intently as their father told them of the foundry in America.

"I'm an old man," he said. "Too old to start over in a foreign land, but you . . ."

The young men looked at each other and then at their father.

Archie, Sr. hung his head. "I did something without asking ye first." He paused and then mumbled, "I wrote to Mr. Pratt."

After a long, awkward silence, Daniel, the eldest, prodded, "And . . ."

"To me surprise, I received a favorable reply from a Mr. Fisher." He held up the note as he danced around the room.

He handed them steamer tickets, packets containing fifty dollars apiece, and train tickets to Montgomery, Alabama, along with a letter of introduction to Mr. Daniel Pratt and Mr. Middleton Fisher from their employer in Scotland.

The three young men sat stunned.

"You've talked about going to America for years," Archie said. "I had a little saved up and," he sputtered, "you'll end up with a miner's cough if you stay here. You deserve better." As he handed the manila envelopes to each boy, he said, "Look for one of the Pratt mule wagons when you get to Montgomery. It'll take you the additional fourteen miles to your new home."

Archie, Sr. cleared his throat and wiped a tear from his cheek. "Pipe smoke!" he snorted and blew his nose. "It reminds me of a Scottish toast."

He raised his glass and saluted each of his boys. "Lang may your lum reek!" he said with pride as his voice cracked.

Adam picked up his glass and saluted the old man. "Long may your chimney smoke, too, Father."

The blast on the Cotton Gin whistle jolted Adam from his thoughts.

"Hurry, children," Sannie said as she shooed the little ones into the courthouse with the palm of her hand.

"Listen to your mother," Adam said as he gave one last hitch to his trousers.

Sannie thought of not wearing a corset today, but she knew if she hadn't, it would be obvious her waist was beginning to swell. She felt the baby kick this morning for the first time. Her emotions were bittersweet as her joy was tempered by the grief of burying her six-month-old baby girl two months earlier. She promised herself she would tell Adam that she was pregnant, but today was his day. It belonged to him and his brothers.

The mass of people inside the large, Georgia pine-paneled room hushed as the plaintiff called out, "All rise! The Honorable Judge J. M. Roy presiding."

Edward, Sannie's twenty-one-year-old brother, leaned closer to Daniel. "So then what happened?" he asked.

"Well," said Daniel with the naturalization document in hand, "the judge read, 'Be it remembered that at ten a.m. on 10 May 1884 in the circuit court of said Autauga County in said State of Alabama, Adam McKay Weir, a native of Scotland, exhibited a petition praying to be admitted to become a citizen of the United States of America' in front of the full assembly."

"And they let him in?" Mr. Fisher said kiddingly. Sannie's adopted father passed cigars to the men crowded in the front parlors of his home to celebrate Adam's big day.

"I'd like to propose a toast," the old man announced as he took a glass of chilled Autauga wine from the tray of his servant, Abraham. The wine, a sweet blend of Scuppernong and Catawba grapes, came as a gift for the occasion from Pratt's private vineyard.

Abraham had been with Sannie's family since before the Civil War. Adisa, the proud name given him by his grandfather at birth, became his middle name, and Abraham, the name he chose from the president who had gained him his freedom, became his first. His grandmother, God rest her soul, chose not to leave the Fisher family. "We be free right here," the old lady told Abraham.

"Adam, you and your brothers came to Prattville twelve years ago, straight off the boat. I let you a room," he said as he placed his hand on Adam's shoulder, "so you could be close to our neighbor, your brother Daniel and his family."

Maggie, his wife, tugged on his arm. "Actually, I let him the room, dear."

He smiled and patted her hand as he continued, "True, but I gave you three a job."

A voice shouted out from the crowd. "Actually, Uncle Pratt gave them a job, Mid," said Merrill Pratt, the current owner of the Cotton Gin Manufactory in town. His uncle's estate had been entrusted to him after Daniel's death in 1873.

"Aye, 'tis true," Mid replied. "But I gave Adam my daughter."

"Actually, I stole her heart," Adam retorted with a laugh.

Mid sighed and smiled. "And you stole ours, as well!"

"Well, then," Mid said to the boys, "to our newest American citizen and to the most loveable son-in-law in our family!"

"Actually, Daddy," Sannie corrected, "he's your only son-in-law until Leonora and Mr. O'Dwyer marry this fall."

"Aye, 'tis true," Mid said with a laugh and raised his glass. "Cheers!" he shouted.

"Cheers," the others replied, and the rooms reverberated with clinking glasses.

"I'd like to say something," Adam said as he stood on Mrs. Fisher's wooden footstool, a drink in one hand and a cigar in the other. He turned to face Mr. Pratt and Mr. Fisher. "Merrill, your uncle, Daniel Pratt, was a remarkable man. He understood that it's not just the job and the pay that's important—"

Adam's brother, Archie, interrupted, "Although they are!" The guests laughed and glasses clinked again.

"Your uncle understood that men *must* be free: to work at what they love; to provide a safe environment for their family; to serve our country; and to help those less fortunate become productive citizens."

Applause broke out in memory of a great man. Every person attending the party had been touched by the generosity of Daniel Pratt, whether it be a job, a loan, or education. He believed in the spirit and goodness of people, and the townsfolk remembered him with great affection.

When the crowd noise subsided, Adam continued. "What a precious gift to own property . . . worship God openly . . . have the right to carry arms . . . speak our minds and move freely in this great land! After all the studying I've done in the last nine years, I've come to the conclusion that the three most perfect documents in the world are: the Bible, the American Constitution, and the Bill of Rights!"

"Adam, now that you're an American, you sound like a politician!" His friends laughed. "When are you going to run for president and which party will you serve?" shouted a voice in the crowd.

"Well, it won't be the Prohibition Party," Adam said as he raised his glass. The crowd broke into cheers and laughter.

"Blaine looks pretty good," said Daniel as he handed Adam another drink. "He certainly stands firm against the Brits."

Merrill Pratt listened intently, "Rumor has it he's taking bribes from the railroad companies. I can't support someone who's involved in shady schemes like that."

Abraham's deep voice could be heard as he moved amongst the crowd. "I ain't votin' for General Sherman! He wise to quit."

Sannie's face registered both surprise and hatred.

Before she could speak, Edward put his arm around his sister and said, "It was in all the papers. Sherman said, 'If drafted, I will not run. If nominated, I will not accept. If elected, I will not serve.'"

Sannie self-consciously raised her fan to cover her pox-marked face.

Daniel's wife, Mary Ellen, asked, "If you could vote for someone, Sannie, who would it be?"

"I'd vote for the Equal Rights Party candidate, Belva Lockwood."

Adam looked at her with surprise. "Why?"

"Because it's women like her that will make it possible for all women to someday have the right to vote, just like freed slaves have had the right since 1876."

That comment started a firestorm of response throughout the crowd. "Not in our lifetime," said someone in the back of the room. "Women are too fragile in thought," whispered another.

Mid asked above the din, "Who's voting for Grover Cleveland?"

Archie, Adam's brother, answered, "I am."

"I'm shocked!" exclaimed Maggie. "Didn't he father a child out of wedlock and now the mother's gone missing?" Another buzz of conversation swept through the room.

"I *was* going to vote for Blaine," yelled someone in a loud voice. "Now, my vote's for Cleveland."

Other partiers responded with a chant of "Mugwump!"

"What's a Mugwump?" Archie asked his brother.

"Well, it means you can't make a decision or don't want to make a decision on your own. You sit on the fence and wait to see which side is winning and then you follow. Your personal position is not based on truth or conviction. It's based on popular opinion. What's a Mugwump? Think of it this way: when you sit on a fence, your mug hangs over one side and your wump over the other."

Sannie loved the wraparound porch on her parent's home. So many lasting memories began right here. A smile passed her lips as she turned to see who had opened the front door.

"There you are," Sannie's mother said. "Miss Julia's been asking for you."

The air was humid and motionless in the approaching evening light. The last rays of sunshine filtered through the newly budded branches on the trees.

"Oh, there you are!" Julia said as she swung the door wide and plopped down on the porch swing next to her sister-in-law.

"Isn't this a wonderful party?" she asked, not really expecting a response.

"Is Colonel Spigener here?" Maggie asked.

"The last I saw of the colonel, he had poor Mr. Northington cornered and was reliving the war years. When he said, 'commanded my troops and something about the war of sections' well, I excused myself to breathe a little of this fresh air. I love my father, but it's hard to talk about a time that caused so much pain for so many! Brother fighting brother, families torn apart."

Sannie placed her hand on her cheek. The beeswax balm hid most of the pox marks she'd received as a young girl when Sherman's troops destroyed the

Fisher family home

plantation and left her family for dead. To this day, she believed the smoldering ashes of the burning corncrib gave her the pox. Never would she admit the visit with her mother to the rebel encampment in the woods behind their estate may have caused her illness. Many of the wounded and dying, waiting to be transported into town, were stricken with fever or chills from infection or disease. Even the sight of freshly dug graves wouldn't change her mind.

Her eyes filled with tears as she thought of her father buried in a similar grave somewhere in Georgia with an unmarked fence post as his headstone. Would they ever know the full story of the battle and his whereabouts? It seemed doubtful.

Julia gasped. "Oh, Miss Sannie, Miss Maggie, I'm so sorry. I didn't mean to bring up such a dreadful subject!" she exclaimed with tears in her eyes.

Maggie Fisher

"It's okay, dear," Maggie said, easing into the large wicker chair next to the porch swing. With a flick of her wrist, her ever-present ivory and lace fan opened. Tiny, well-placed flips close to her face cooled the perspiration on her neck.

"I know something we can talk about that's much happier," she said as she closed the fan with a snap and placed it on her lap. She looked directly at her daughter.

Sannie looked back, suspecting the news somehow involved her. "What?"

"Sannie, when are you going to tell us?" Maggie said and paused, studying the young woman's face. Her firstborn gave no hint.

With hands on hips, Maggie leaned forward and asked, "When are you going to tell us . . . you're having a baby?"

"How did you know?"

Julia looked shocked. "Then it's true!"

Sannie asked again, "How did you know?"

"My dear," her mother said with a laugh, "every time you're with child, you have this sweet little habit of rubbing your tummy."

Sannie pulled her hand away from her belly with a giggle and said, "I do not!"

"Does Adam know?" Julia asked.

"No," Sannie said.

Her mother gave her that look again.

"What!"

Maggie shook her head. "It was Adam who told me about your little quirk."

"He knows? Why didn't he say something?"

Maggie answered Sannie's question with one of her own. "Why didn't you?"

Even though Sannie's glance toward Oak Hill Cemetery was brief, Maggie knew. . . .

"Your precious little baby was sick with fever, sweetheart," her mother said quietly, knowing the pain her daughter felt.

"Oh, Mama, every time I think of this sweet child growing inside me, I think of my little girl."

Abraham's wife, Linda, opened the door slightly. The conversation drifting from the parlors confirmed the men were *still* talking politics.

"Even if Grover Cleveland has a bastard child, it doesn't mean he's not the best man for the job," a voice shouted above the din.

Someone responded mockingly with the imposing party's slogan, "Mama, where's my pa?"

The crowd answered in unison, "In the White House, ha-ha-ha."

"Miss Ma'git, we ready to serve dinner now," Linda said.

Maggie looked at the two women. "Please tell the men we'll be in soon."

"Yes, ma'am."

Julia held Sannie's hand and said, "I miss my son, too, Miss Sannie. "Mid was fourteen years old when he died in that dreadful accident!"

(l–r): William Middleton (son of Middleton Davis Fisher), Margarite, young Mid, Julia (Spigener) Fisher, and housekeeper, Linda.

Maggie said gently but firmly, "Now, I want you two to listen to me. There are no guarantees to the length of our life on this earth. Losing a child at any age is the greatest pain a parent will ever endure."

Maggie bit her lower lip, looked toward Oak Hill Cemetery, and said, "I was pregnant with your brother when your father was killed. The baby was born ailing. He was so frail when we moved from Georgia to Alabama. I blamed myself for him not being strong enough to survive."

"Mama, I never knew," Sannie replied.

Maggie cupped her daughter's face in her hands. "You were but a child yourself."

"The nanny who tended to me was a negro lady. Some folks say her mama was Creek, but I don't know if that's true or not. The Indians pretty much stayed to themselves on the outskirts of town near Cooter's Pond. I'll never forget Chatty Washington," Maggie said with a smile of gratitude upon her face.

"Miss Maggie?" she said in hushed tones as she bent over my bed. "I have a present for you and your sweet little Angel Baby."

"The orange glow from the flames of the fireplace magnified her kind face," Maggie recalled. "Chatty was wide of girth with a complexion the color of molasses. A handful of nappy hair peeked beyond the kerchief on her head. Chatty smelled of clove and apple and pine. The scent came from a medicine bag hung on a leather cord around her neck with a snake's rattle neatly sewn on the pouch."

"You knows Miss Hagerty?" Chatty asked. Her hand caressed an ornately engraved cylinder resting on her lap. "This come from Scotland. Mr. Hagerty? He be a sea man."

"And with that, Chatty laid the kaleidoscope in my arms," Maggie said as her arms gestured toward the girls.

"Here," said Chatty. "This be the story of life."

"What did you do?" Julia asked.
"I twisted the top as Miss Chatty instructed."
"And what did you see?" Sannie asked.

"I'd never seen anything like it! The tiny pieces of colored glass formed delicate patterns more intricate and vibrant than a stained-glass window."

"It keeps changing," I told her.

"Just like life," Chatty said, and with that, she was gone."

"I remember you looking at that kaleidoscope for hours when I was a child," Sannie said.

"Every time I twisted it, I learned more."

"How so, Miss Maggie?" Julia asked.

"The colors in the patterns took on the personalities of members in our family. Each time I looked at the patterns and they changed, it reminded me of how beautiful and fragile we all are."

Sannie thought before responding, "Just like the pieces of glass, we build our own patterns in life."

"Yes," Maggie replied in agreement. "We may not fully grasp why a baby or child is taken from us, and we'll wonder until our last breath. Suffice it to know that the family's pattern is complete because they lived . . . no matter how brief."

Maggie patted her daughter's hand. "There are times it feels like chaos, and we respond with fear or anger or despair because we don't understand. We only see the full beauty of the pattern when we realize there's a larger picture, and we are but one piece—an important piece, but none the less, only one."

"One twist and a new generation begins," Sannie said, oblivious that her hand tenderly rubbed her belly.

"All the colors are still there," Julia added.

Maggie took a sip of iced tea and added, "Even though it's a new generation in an evolving pattern, it's solidly built on the past."

"Patterns ebb and flow, but the overall beauty remains," Maggie said. "It's all part of a Master Plan."

The heat of the day began to wane. Crickets chirped their nightly chorus as twilight settled in.

"I promise you," Maggie added with conviction, "we will celebrate every precious life God gives to us and remember each one for the joy and talent and mischief they've brought into this world and left in our hearts."

Without warning, the door burst open and out poured Adam and Daniel and Archie draped in red, white, and blue bunting. Middleton followed, chomping on a cigar.

The women looked at this motley parade of revelers and burst into laughter.

"I think we know the colors of this generation," Maggie laughed.

"Ladies!" Middleton announced while ringing the dinner bell furiously. "Dinner is served."

CHAPTER 4

1902

Mile High Dreams

It was the beginning of October in Colorado. A flurry of gold leaves from the quaking aspens blew to the ground on the stiff northerly breeze.

"I'm glad we had a chance to walk through the old Empson cannery last night before this storm rolled in," Adam said as he tucked his hands into his coat pockets. "I'm looking forward to meeting Mr. Empson this morning, but dang, it's cold!"

"Are you sure about this?" Mid asked as he pulled his coat closer to his chest and pushed into the door at the Past Time Café on Main Street. A gust caught a stack of receipts on the end of the counter and hurled them into the air as the door shut with a thunk.

"I thought you put those papers away!" Patty shouted to her husband as she salvaged the ones that landed on the floor.

"Sorry, honey, the delivery wagon pulled up and I got sidetracked," Robert replied apologetically. He helped his wife pick up the rest of the slips of paper.

Middleton and Adam slid into an empty booth next to a window. The cold from outside seeped into the crevices around the pane of glass and caused a halo of fog around the frame, creating a Currier and Ives view of the mountains beyond.

"You boys new to the area or just passing through?" Patty asked. She had the coffee pot poised to pour, and both men gratefully moved their cups to the edge of the table.

The breakfast regulars hushed, straining to learn more about the strangers.

"We came in last night," Mid answered.

"Prospectors?" she asked. Middleton and Adam both sported beards that covered most of their chests.

"No, ma'am," said Adam. "I'm placing a bid on the old Empson cannery on Fourteenth."

A flood of whispers spilled through the diner.

"And do what?" asked Robert as he joined his wife at the table, his hands holding a ledger and the pile of unpaid bills.

"Open a foundry."

"A foundry, eh?" Robert mused and slipped the papers onto a shelf under the counter.

Steam rose from the cup warming Middleton Fisher's hands. He took a long sip and sighed, "Ahhhhh . . . that tastes good."

"How 'bout some breakfast to go with that?" Patty prompted, her order pad in hand.

"That old building would be perfect for a foundry," Robert said. "Have you talked to the Grand Junction Fruit Growers Association in Grand Valley? When their equipment breaks down, it's a trip to Denver," he said as he threw his hands in the air. "We have a blacksmith in town for small jobs, but a foundry! What a godsend that would be."

He sat down next to the two men, and after making sure no one could hear their conversation, said, "Look . . . my cousin's a grower beyond the Big Salt Wash west of Fruita, 65 acres in peaches and 110 in apples."

Robert scribbled a note on a piece of paper and slipped it to Adam. "Rumor has it Mesa County's installing an irrigation system for the orchards. Give him a call."

"What made you decide on Grand Junction?" Patty asked as she placed their food on the table. "By the way, that's Empson's Silver Kettle currant jelly," she said as she placed the jar in front of them.

"Thank you, ma'am," Adam replied.

He slathered his toast and thought about what Patty asked before answering her. "I like the proximity to the rail lines, for one thing. Between the growers, the miners, the ranchers, and the changes in home cooking, I see a lot of opportunity here."

"Weather's refreshing," Middleton chuckled with a mischievous wink.

They laughed as they watched the dust and tumbleweed blow down the street.

"Morning," the pleasant-looking man said to Robert with a tip of his hat. He brushed the dust from his coat and cleaned the dirt from his spectacles before acknowledging the waitress with a brief nod.

"Morning, John," Robert replied.

"Good morning, gentlemen," Mr. Empson said as he studied the two strangers. "I believe we have business to discuss."

Patty placed a full pot of coffee on the table as the man slid into the booth.

Adam stood in the doorway of Middleton's office at the foundry in Prattville, holding an unopened envelope in his hand.

It was eight weeks since their visit to Colorado. Empson seemed a man of honor, and the two men agreed to do business on a handshake.

"Come in . . . close the door," Middleton said in hushed tones. Together, they scanned the bill of sale.

"Adam," he exclaimed with excitement and joy, "you're now the proud owner of the—the—" Mid paused, realizing he was at a loss for words. "What did you name it?"

"The Western Slope Foundry," Adam said, grinning from ear to ear. He plopped into the overstuffed chair in the corner of the office and read the document again.

"Good job, son. All your hard work and perseverance paid off. You followed your dream. Now, it's up to you to get out there and make it work for you."

A tone of sadness edged Mid's words. As much as he supported his son-in-law's vision, he knew it meant the family would be separated. He may never see his daughter again.

"When do you and Sannie plan on leaving?" he asked.

"Sometime in June," Adam said quietly. "About eight months from now."

Sannie didn't want to let go of her mother's hand.

"All aboard!" the conductor shouted. He stood on the step of the passenger car and signaled the engineer in the cab of the locomotive with a swing of his lantern. The train's wheels began to turn slowly, with a screech of metal slipping on metal. Billows of smoke and steam belched from the stack. The horn, a jarring jolt of noise that replaced the wail of the whistle three years ago, sounded two short warning blasts.

"I'll write as soon as we get to Colorado," Sannie said through her tears.

"Give those little ones a hug from me every night," her mother cried as she blew kisses to her grandchildren.

"Archie's going to find me an arrowhead," four-year-old Palmer told his father, Daniel, "and a gold nugget!" The child patted his father's cheeks, drying the man's tears. "It's okay, Daddy. I'll share my gold with you."

Adam stood on the stairs of the train with the conductor. He realized, as he waved to Daniel and Archie, that he might never see his brothers again. The lump in his throat made it hard to swallow. Had they made the right decision?

His job with Pratt was secure. The family was well-respected pillars of the community. They were comfortable and established. If it weren't for that nagging cough and continual warnings from the doctor, "Move to a drier climate or risk consumption," they'd live out their lives in Prattville and spend eternity at Oak Hill Cemetery in the family plot. They loved Alabama.

Adam and Sannie's extended family huddled at the end of the wooden platform, wishing their loved ones well. Smiles and waves masked the tears of the adults as the children played hide-and-seek around the piles of luggage.

No more family meals on Sunday or sitting on the Fisher's front porch in the evening. No more celebrations and good-hearted teasing between cousins. No more gatherings in happy times and sad. It was a high price for good health—higher still to follow Adam's dream.

The train sounded one last blast. The massive wheels churned and strained against the iron rails; metal ground upon metal. The family left behind stared at the empty tracks until the last curl of smoke and steam evaporated on the horizon. Then the well-wishers from the platform crowded into their buggies and headed for home as the family members on the train took their seats and watched the scenery and their lives change before their eyes.

CHAPTER 5

1916

Prophecy

Midnight . . . and all was still. Trudi and the children left hours ago. Sannie smiled as she thought of her growing family. How quickly her children turned into young men and women with families of their own. Had it really been fourteen years since she and Adam left Prattville for a new life on the western slope of the Rockies in Grand Junction, Colorado?

Adam and Sannie's whole life revolved around family and faith. His dream of owning a business to secure the financial future of his sons had been realized. She felt blessed to have her married children living close by: Archie and Trudi in one direction; Murray and Edith in the other; Maria, Bernice, and their spouses one town over. Their house was filled with kids and laughter and good times . . . until the boys got to drinking.

Sannie stared at the bedroom ceiling, unable to sleep. The streetlight cast harsh shadows through the window, which magnified her angry thoughts. An hour passed, then another. She rolled to her side and watched Adam's chest slowly fill with air as he slept undisturbed. His white beard lay like a blanket of snow upon his chest.

Sannie heard Archie's mule bray in the front yard and knew the boys were home. A returned whicker followed from a horse in the public corral up the street.

"Shhhhhhhh!" Wil cautioned, stumbling up the porch stairs with his brother, Murray, hanging on his arm. "You're goin' ta wake Ma," he slurred.

"We don't want to do that!" Murray whispered back.

"I'm already awake," Sannie said as she turned on the ceiling light in the living room.

Murray winced and lifted his head. "Is it time for work? I don't think I slept all night."

"Where's your brother?" she asked.

The boys pointed at each other.

"I'm in no mood for your shenanigans. When you left, there were three of you. Now, where is Archie?!"

"He was at—UH!" Murray groaned when he felt Wil's elbow jab him in the ribs.

"Ma, I—I don't remember," he stammered.

"You two are worthless when you're drunk, and you're drunk more than not! It's pretty sad when a mother can only get an honest answer from a jackass!"

Sannie grabbed her coat from the rack and seized the whip. The door slammed shut, and Murray grabbed for the horseshoe over the doorjamb as it leapt off the wall.

Wil let out a low whistle. "I don't think I ever saw Ma so mad."

The boys scrambled for the window and watched the lone silhouette of the sixty-year-old woman hunched over from the chill night air, wheeling toward Main Street.

I'll bet Archie and the boys are sorry they ever taught this little mule to play hide-and-seek, Sannie thought as she settled into the box on the buckboard.

"Let's go!" she clucked. "Black Jack, find Archie!" The faithful little creature headed for the Past Time Café at a nice clip. Black Jack knew *his* reward was a carrot. It didn't matter whose hand held it.

Sannie pulled into the cobblestone alley. Music, voices, and the clink of glasses could be heard as she opened the door.

"You can't go in there," the brawny man said as he stepped in front of the tiny woman.

"I've raised nine kids and survived the Civil War. Do you really think you're going to stop me?" Sannie asked as she gave the bullwhip one hearty crack. The place went silent.

The bartender looked at his watch and then yelled, "Archie! Your mom's here."

"Aw, jeesh, Ma!" Archie said before he chugged the last of the whiskey in his glass. "Can't a guy let off a little steam?"

Sannie stood with her arms crossed over her chest. Her four-foot-eleven frame stood squarely in front of Archie's stool. Her violet eyes flashed with anger.

Unflinching, she looked at the bartender. "Sam?"

He obediently responded, "Yes, ma'am?"

He'd seen Sannie pull a drink off a table with that whip. Last year, it cost him $123.42 in broken glass. A small fortune taken from a working man's $1.50 an hour wage, but he was glad to pay it if it kept the word of his after-hours business from reaching the ears of his boss, the owner of the café. If Sannie reported it, Sam would be out of a job, or worse yet, in jail.

"I don't want no trouble, Miss Sannie."

She pushed her hand under his nose. "Then give me Archie's earnings and help me get him in the buckboard. Anything left in his keg?" she asked.

"Nah. It's pretty much tapped out. He's a generous guy. Customers like it when someone shares, especially in this dry state," the bartender replied.

"I'd appreciate it if you would stop selling to him," she said.

"We don't sell liquor in Colorado—or Utah, for that matter."

"How's he getting it?" she asked.

"Fur traders, prospectors, even Indians from New Mexico use liquor for barter at the outposts."

Sannie knew her son spent a lot of time in the mountains, but one thing she didn't know and only Sam could answer was: "How are you making money on this, Sam?"

"The way the law's written, I can't sell alcohol to you, but you bring a bottle or keg to me and we'll store it for you. Any time you'd like a drink, we'll give you a glass for a small fee and you serve yourself."

"I knew I should've broken more of those glasses," Sannie said as she raised the whip above her head.

With a nod of his head, Sam motioned to the bouncer, and the two of them quickly muscled Archie's limp body into the buckboard. Sannie guided the wagon through the open fields on Pitkin Street so Archie felt every rut and swale on the journey home. Thistles and briars clung to the back of his pant legs as his bootheels dragged along the ground. The little burro's hooves, muted by the dirt trail, didn't awaken the neighbors.

Sannie gently thunked Archie on the side of the head with the butt of the whip.

"Ow! Uhhhh . . . Ma, take it easy!"

"A little rap on the noggin isn't going to hurt you, son. I'm hoping it'll knock some sense into you," she said.

"Can we talk about this in the morning?"

"No. I'll talk; you listen." She turned to look at him lying in the back of the buckboard and saw he'd passed out again. She thumped the handle of the whip on the flooring and watched him wince.

"Maaaaa," Archie murmured, grimacing from the noise.

"I had a long talk with Trudi this evening. She's had it with you, and so have I."

"Ahhhhh," Archie sighed with frustration.

"You're throwing your life away, son," Sannie said with a lump in her throat. "It's breaking your father's heart knowing how the business he started for you and your brothers is facing hard times, and some of the responsibility falls on your shoulders."

Archie raised up. "Ma, everybody's suffering from the recession."

Sannie pointed her finger at him. "I know better! I've gone through the books and looked at the correspondence. You and your brothers are sliding by on your father's good name. He's an old man. It's time for you to step up!" she hissed. The fury she'd been holding in boiled to the surface.

"You have a wife and a family!" she said with tears in her eyes. "Trudi was here this afternoon asking for food money. Food money!" she said again to emphasize her point. "You bought how many drinks for strangers tonight, and your boys would have gone to bed without dinner if I hadn't given her *food* money!"

Gertrude "Trudi" Ethel Pasley

"Ma, she—" Archie began

to say in his own defense.

"Hush! There is nothing you have to say right now that I want to hear." Sannie's fists clenched the reins as though she were driving a runaway stagecoach. "Archie Middleton Weir, you are a scoundrel! You spend weeks and months on the mountains looking for gold . . . chasing pipe dreams! You literally throw your money down the hole of the crapper with all you drink. You have two little boys who need their father. If you don't change your ways, someday—maybe not this month or next, maybe not next year or the one after that—but someday something will happen and you'll lose your family, your money, maybe even your life."

Archie did not respond except with a snore. Sannie bent over the wooden seat and wept.

Quietly, she pulled the cart into Archie's backyard. A gentle autumn rain had begun to fall. She took the harness off Black Jack, led him into the open pen, and walked the two blocks home.

From her bedroom window, Sannie could see Archie's legs hanging off the end of the buckboard. Trudi was silhouetted by a glimmer of light as she opened the kitchen door. She pulled her shawl from her shoulders and covered her husband's unconscious body. Her two young boys watched from the doorway until she shooed them back in the house.

Another day . . .

Archie Middleton Weir

CHAPTER 6

1924

Promises . . . Promises

Trudi watched as Archie set the packs on the backs of Lucky Charm and Jack Pot for the trek into backcountry. Black Jack, his favorite burro, paced the length of the paddock. He loved to be on the trail. "Not this time, buddy. You've got to rest that leg," Archie said as he scratched the burro's ear.

"Just a couple of nights, Trudi. When I come back, I'll place a nugget the size of an apple in the palm of your hand," Archie said as he tightened the pack animal's girth strap.

How many times had she heard these Mountain Fever rants? Last year alone, ten thousand prospectors rushed to stake a claim on raw land in Colorado and moved on with a sprinkling of gold dust and a pocketful of unfulfilled dreams. Deep in her heart, she prayed this time would be different for her husband, for her, for their children. If anyone could find that pay shoot, it would be Archie. After all, he had lived in this area since he was a young man. He knew the mountains. He knew the locals. He knew metals and minerals and how to analyze his findings.

It was an hour before dawn. It would take till noon to reach the trailhead . . . maybe longer. There was talk in town of a gulley washer near Owl Creek Pass. Partially submerged and dislodged boulders the size of a watering trough posed a challenge for prospector and pack animal alike. Trudi pulled his bedroll, hand lens, gold pans, and extra shovel handles closer to the porch steps.

"I need to talk to you, Trudi, before I go," Archie said with a seriousness she had not heard before. "Come here," he said, motioning to the bale of hay next to the paddock fence.

Streaks of purple and pink in the morning sky accentuated the mountain's ridgelines. The chill morning air cut through Trudy's cotton nightdress, causing a shiver. She drew her shawl closer.

Archie put his arms around his wife. He loved her dearly. She was a good woman: sensible, loyal. "Trudi, I've made a map. I've torn it into three sections. Keep this portion in a safe place. I've hidden one part at the foundry. The final piece, I'm sending to Grandpa Fisher. If anything happens to me—"

Trudi and Archie

"Happen! What are you talking about?"

"It's only a precaution," Archie said as he kissed the back of her neck. His breath reeked of stale whiskey.

"You're talking crazy!" she said as she wriggled out of his grasp.

"Maybe," he replied. His eyes scanned the horizon. He knew he had to leave soon or face a blazing sun. Blue shadows bathed the western slope. Spots of color came alive when the sun crested the ridges to the east, spilling fingers of light into the valleys.

"Bob Vitarill's been nosing around, asking questions. Word has it, Mike MacFarlane accused him of claim jumping a year back, and now nobody's heard from MacFarlane."

"Curious thing is," Archie added, "Vitarill's spending a lot more time at the assayer's office."

"What does this have to do with you?"

"Nothing really. I just don't trust him. If anything happens to me, keep an eye on Vitarill." Archie spread the map piece on his lap. "Remember when we went to Camp Johnson on Pinon Mesa with your sister and her husband?"

Gertrude replied with a slow nod of her head. "Why?" she asked cautiously.

"We talked about hitting it big someday, remember? Well . . . this is it."

She looked at him and shook her head.

"I know you've heard it all before,

Camp Johnson, Pinon Mesa, CO

but hear me out." He pointed to a scribble of tiny circles on the map. "Remember that waterfall where the black swifts darted so quickly we could barely see them?"

She thought a moment. "You could see Twin Peaks in the distance," she replied.

"Yes," Archie nodded with excitement.

"We were surrounded by wildflowers on that grassy knoll near Black Bear Pass."

"The trailhead is here, Trudi." Archie pointed to a spot not far from the falls. "I found placer gold in the creek bed's silt. Not far upstream, I dug into the mountain and found a narrow vein running into hard rock. It looks good!"

Trudi's mouth opened. She didn't know whether to laugh or cry. She grabbed Archie by the arms. "Are you sure?"

He laughed and swung her around the yard. "Sure enough to stake a claim on it!"

Trudi stopped abruptly, causing Archie to stumble over her skirt and land on his haunches. "What's the matter?" he asked, shaking the dust from his hat.

"Where did you get money to stake a claim?"

"Don't worry about that. It's all been taken care of," he said, realizing he had told her too much.

Trudi stood over him and asked again slowly, "Where . . . did . . . you . . . get . . . the . . . money?"

With a long sigh, Archie replied, "I got it from my brothers, okay?"

With arms crossed, Trudi said, "And?"

"And what?" he answered, feigning innocence. "There is no *and*."

"And what did you give them in return?" she asked.

"I'm not giving them anything, Trudi. When I come back, I'll pay off my shares . . ."

"What shares?" she demanded. Archie went silent.

Archie tightened the cinch on Jack Pot's pack.

"Archie, what have you done?"

"I've done something that will keep you farting in silk bloomers for the rest of your life!" he shouted.

Trudi sat on the front steps, rocking back and forth. "You owe a fortune on the foundry you bought a year ago. I've almost paid off your bar tab up the street with the laundry I take in. And what do you do? You give away our only source of security. You squandered our future. Our kids' future! For what?"

"For a better life, Trudi," Archie responded defensively as he tied his bedroll onto Jack Pot. "You'll see. When I get back, you'll see."

———

A dusting of snow covered the back of the animal's hide. Downwind of the creature and out of direct sight, Vitarill slowly drew his pistol as the animal shuddered and rolled. "One. Two.

Three," the mountain man slowly counted under his breath. He let out a whoop and charged.

Startled, the animal rose, then fell to the ground. Archie stood in its place, revolver in hand. "Drop it!" he yelled. The barrel of his Colt .45 pointed at Vitarill's heart.

"Holy Mother, what are you doing?!" Vitarill yelled back, throwing his weapon to his feet and raising his hands above his head.

Archie slumped into a fetal position, pants pulled down, exposing his swollen buttock.

Vitarill picked up his weapon and walked toward the wounded man.

"Black widow in the hole of the crapper," Archie said, his voice weak, throat parched. He pulled the hide over his shoulder with a groan as the raw edge tore across the open wound on his backside.

"How long you been like this?" Vitarill asked.

"Don't know."

"You're lucky to be alive!"

Archie's hands shook as he dug a piece of chewing tobacco from his pouch and tucked it in his cheek. He took a swill of whiskey, chewed the mash, spat it in his hand, and pressed the poultice onto the oozing sore.

"We need to get you off this mountain," Vitarill said, looking at the boulder-strewn mud path.

"Can't walk. Burros gone," Archie rasped as he crawled back under the hide for warmth.

"I saw them half a mile down the face, near the bend in the river. There's a sluice box down there. Is that yours?" he asked.

"I have a claim to this land," Archie said with ice in his voice. "You're trespassing."

"Don't mean nothin' by it," Vitarill said, backing away.

Archie recalled the disappearance of MacFarlane and the rumors of Vitarill's involvement and said nothing more.

"When did you last eat?" Vitarill asked.

"Dunno."

"You stay here," Vitarill said. "I'm gonna set a couple of traps and round up the animals. Here's some jerky and hardtack. Eat it," he commanded. "I'll be back," he added and disappeared.

If it weren't for the hardtack in hand, Archie reasoned Vitarill's visit to be another hallucination. Partially paralyzed from the spider's venom, he slowly dragged himself towards the mule's pack and a fresh canteen of whiskey.

The cedars swayed in the early morning breeze, mimicking the sound of the river's current. Roots hugged bare rock on the sheer wall of the mountain a few feet from Archie's pine needle bed. A pain pierced his arm as a jagged limb tore at his shirt. Terrified, Archie shouted in fear as the tentacles in his mind pulled him toward the netherworld. He shielded his eyes against the vision of falling rocks burying him alive.

"Stop!" he wailed in agony. The sound of his voice echoed off the canyon walls.

Archie's screams reached Vitarill's ears a quarter mile away. As he turned his donkey around to begin the trek back to the injured man's camp, he heard hysterical laughter and a man baying like a crazed coyote and realized Archie was doing as best he could in his delusional state. Vitarill continued his journey.

It was a 1,500-foot drop to the ground from the parapet where he knelt. He reverently placed the doeskin hide on the flat stone altar. Veins of pyrite, flecks of fools gold, and chips of quartz glistened in the sunlight. "Dominus Vobiscum," the priest said with a sweep of his outstretched hands over the vast horizon and valley below. His six-foot-eight frame reached heavenward. His eyes closed in prayer.

Vitarill and his fellow priest, MacFarlane, wandered the towns and mountaintops from Silverton to Ouray to Telluride, bringing the promise of salvation and the words of Christ to pioneers, miners, and prospectors. Last year, MacFarlane had been abruptly summoned to the Holy See in Baltimore. Vitarill missed his friend. MacFarlane's easygoing, jovial personality put everyone at ease. Vitarill secretly envied this trait. MacFarlane used his gift to befriend people before sharing his calling with them. "People are more apt to talk to me about the serious stuff when they know I care for them as a human being, warts and all," he would say.

Vitarill finished his morning ritual and closed with a brief prayer. "God send the Holy Spirit to guide my tongue. Help me to do your will."

In the flicker of the evening fire, shadows from the trees and foliage jumped around the campsite, leaving monstrous apparitions in the mind of the demented man. Archie cried out in his altered state. Vitarill comforted him as best he could and stayed by his side for the next five days.

"Something smells good," Archie said during a lucid moment. "It's rabbit and flatbread," Vitarill replied. "I'll get you a plate."

He propped himself up on his good side and stared into the embers. His muscles were weak and bones stiff, but the fever was gone.

"What's the date?" he asked as he realized there were patches of new grass where snow once laid.

"It's around the end of May or the first part of June," Vitarill answered. "Why?"

"Just wondering," he said with an ache in his heart to be with his family. "My son's birthday's the eighth of May. He'll be twelve this year."

"Would that be Tom?" Vitarill asked.

"My younger son," Archie replied. "How did you know his name?" Archie asked curiously, suspecting the man had rummaged through his things.

"You kept telling him to finish his homework. I take it he doesn't like school."

"He hates it!" Archie said. "This summer, he'll apprentice with me in the foundry like I did with my father and he did with his in Scotland."

"Scotland! My partner's from Glasgow . . . MacFarlane. Do you know him?" Vitarill asked.

"Haven't seen him 'round for about a year. Some say he found the mother lode and was taken out by claim jumpers," Archie said, watching the mountain man's every move.

Vitarill let out a hearty laugh.

"What's so funny?" Archie asked, stunned by his reaction.

"MacFarlane took a vow of poverty," he said, noting Archie's look of utter surprise. "You didn't know? He's a priest! The reason you haven't seen him in these parts is because he was summoned back east."

Archie's eyes widened. "You said you're partners. . . . You're a priest?"

Vitarill nodded his head and smiled.

"I thought you were one of the claim jumpers."

The giant man laughed until he snorted.

"Why are you always at the assayer's office?" Archie asked.

"Because he's married to my sister."

Archie slapped himself upside the head and began to laugh. "Now it all makes sense! Jeez, you two got a lot of busy bees stirred up in town."

"MacFarlane used to say, 'Let people say what they want. They'll learn the power of truth over gossip and the repercussions of gossip quicker that way.'"

"What else did I talk about?" Archie asked, fearing what he may have said.

A sober look came over Vitarill's face. "You promised your mother and your wife, if you survived this, you'd take the pledge."

Archie looked at the whiskey in his cup and defensively said, "I can stop anytime I want. I just happen to like the taste of it. You know how women get, especially teetotalers."

Vitarill stroked his beard and was quiet for a long time. "That spider bite was pretty potent, but from what I saw, I'd say you also wrestled with the DTs. If you've made it this far, why not go the rest of the way and give that blasted family-wrecking hooch the boot?"

"I don't see where it's causing a problem," Archie said defensively as he took a swill.

"Do you and your wife argue over it?" Vitarill asked.

"We argue over everything," Archie answered.

"Do you miss work?"

"I've never missed a day," Archie said proudly.

"Do you feel like hell when you're there? Is it hard to concentrate? Has anybody hinted that you're not carrying your load?"

"Hey, I work with my brothers. I'm the eldest. There's always going to be times when they don't see it my way." Archie was becoming agitated. "What's your point, Vitarill?"

"The point is . . . what causes a problem is one," Vitarill said firmly as he rested his back against a boulder. He folded his hands and closed his eyes before quietly adding, "I'm not asking you to stop. I'm asking you to think of the choices you've made and really reflect on the impact they're having on you and your family."

A full moon hung low in the sky, slow-dancing across the jagged peaks. A glimmer of soft light blanketed the landscape.

"Did you ever see anything more beautiful?" the priest asked, struck with awe.

"Maybe a nugget the size of an apple," Archie said with a chuckle.

"Those are few and far between! Find one yet?"

"Naw."

"How long you been looking?"

"Started panning when I was twenty," Archie said. He thought a moment and added, "About twenty-two years."

"That's a long time. Most men would have stopped by now."

"When I'm down there," Archie said, pointing toward town, "I'm counting the days before I'm back on the mountain. I paid a fortune for a claim on two parcels of land this time. I was so sure . . ." Archie hung his head and quietly said, "I lost my family's savings."

"That's tough," Father Vitarill replied.

"You don't understand. I talked my brothers into going in on this with me, I was so sure."

"Why?"

"Jeez, you sound just like my wife!" Archie sighed. "These mountains are filled with gold. Just one lucky strike and we are set for life."

"Archie, you have a loving family, a secure job, and your health. I'd say you're already a blessed man. Wealth is not going to buy you inner peace or happiness. That only comes from knowing our Lord," Vitarill said. "If you want to find true gold, start digging in here," the priest said as he thumped his finger on the cover of the Bible.

Archie and the holy man sat in silence, staring at the last of the embers and the occasional spark. Archie swigged the last of the whiskey in his canteen.

"I'll be leaving in the morning," Vitarill said. "I think you're well enough to make it to town. I'll keep you and your family in my prayers." He threw the remnants from the coffee pot onto the campfire's ashes and crawled into his bedroll. "Stop in and see my sister from time to time. Let her know how you're doing. I'll get the message."

"Good night, Father."

"Good night, Archie. God bless."

After a night of foraging, a herd of mule deer returned to the forest near Archie's campsite as the last of the evening stars submitted to the early morning light. Vitarill was gone. The distant call of a bull elk echoed through the ravine. Archie slowly pulled his hat over his face. His head throbbed from too much whiskey. Today he was breaking camp. Tomorrow was the day of reckoning. How would he face Trudi? His brothers? How would he explain?

He laid his head on his rolled-up poncho and began to doze until the sound of hooves coming his way woke him with a jolt. Stones and dust hit Archie square in the chest. He scrambled to his feet, gun drawn.

"Dammit, Lucky! One of these days you're going to take a slug right between the eyes."

The little burro let out a long, honking bray, shook its head, and started down the mountainous path.

Even he knew it was time to head home.

CHAPTER 7

1924

Innocence Lost

Creeks burgeoned with fresh runoff from melting snow in the San Juan Mountains. Below the timberline, spring flowers danced in meadows and dressed the cliffs and crevices with splashes of brilliant color. Archie and Trudi moved from Grand Junction to Ouray to begin anew. The postcard-perfect town was a few hours south and east from the rest of the family. That was three years ago.

"We'll make a clean start of it," he promised her.

Trudi worked as a cook at Camp Bird before the couple opened the foundry last year. Camp Bird, named for the vibrant blue birds that called the twelve thousand-foot mountain home. The active quarry produced long drifts of silver that drew prospectors to town from all over the nation.

"If that mountaintop is rich with ore, then there's more nearby" was the first chill of gold rush fever, and thousands were afflicted.

When you sit on the back of a pack animal, you learn to trust the beast's sure-footedness on the narrow paths, and you learn to duck to avoid low-lying branches that slap and grab unsuspecting riders not vigilant to the terrain. One slip toward the rushing water from the gorge one hundred feet below, and eyes are forever opened wide to the perils of mountain travel.

Trudi on the trail to Camp Bird

Trudi occasionally passed a foolhardy tenderfoot or a carriage overflowing with celebrities anticipating the thrill of the wild, wild west on this hazardous route. Carts and wagons pitched from side to side in the carved ruts, and unsuspecting greenhorns squealed with excitement until they became mired in muck and had to push the wagon down the trail towards civilization.

On her final ride from the mine a year ago, the path abruptly halted, strewn with felled trees from a late spring avalanche. A stand of eighty-foot cedars littered the mountainside near the bend at the halfway point. Trunk circumferences, the size of small wagons, lay snapped at the root base. Trees pitched downward like pieces from the child's game of pick-up-sticks. She'd heard rumors that lumberjacks and townsmen spent the better part of a month clearing a small passageway for those needing to travel to and from the mine, but this was her first encounter.

An eerie quiet enveloped the area. The thunder of the rapids hushed, birds silenced their songs . . . not even a bray from Black Jack. It was as though all creatures recognized this one-mile path of destruction was a warning to all living things great and small: Respect the power of Mother Nature in all her majesty and fury. We are mere visitors in an unforgiving environment.

Trudi hugged her coat closely around her body, glad to be back in town. She no longer worried about avalanche-blocked trails, or worse, landslides through camp in the middle of night.

She was proud of her sons, fourteen-year-old Spike (a childhood nickname for her firstborn and Archie's namesake), and his younger brother, twelve-year-old Tom. She could rely on them to get ready for school, even though she wasn't there to prod them. Every sunup, she'd pack their lunches before leaving for the foundry situated at the base of Box Canyon, near Canyon Creek on the edge of town.

"Be good boys," she'd say as she closed the door behind her. "I love you more than time can tell!"

She'd glance in the direction of the trail to Camp Bird and recall the stands of pine, cedar, and aspen that shadowed the treacherous pass, the tight switchbacks and sheer drop-offs winding through the Alpine tundra. She was grateful the foundry was an easy four-block walk from their apartment.

She had tired of traveling the six miles by mule or on foot with two young boys in tow. Winters, snowed-in on the mountaintop, created hardships for the boys. Only a handful of children, and little besides chores to do, caused long bouts of cabin fever.

Archie had opened the foundry on Third Street last summer. He was a new man—promised to change his ways, again. Settle down this time. No more drinking . . . he promised.

The apprentice Archie hired was already busy at the kiln when Trudi arrived. She walked to the office in the back of the building and opened the window facing Canyon creek. Murky water filled the stream, a polluted runoff from miners upstream, who used the rivulet to wash through the sludge that held tailings of silver and the occasional gold nugget from Camp Bird. Oh, how she hated the fascination of gold!

"Just one more trip up the mountain, Trudi," Archie told her. That was three weeks ago.

"Come on, Tom," Spike yelled as he waited on the front steps. "We're going to be late!"

Tom at 12 years old

Tom tucked his slingshot in the back pocket of his britches as he yelled back to his brother, "You go ahead. I'm meeting up with Danny."

It was the end of the school year, and the temptation to visit the swimming hole, nestled in the Uncompaghe Gorge, overcame the two twelve-year-old boys. Danny and Tom had been best pals for almost two years now. Inseparable, their parents said.

Spike didn't know Tom was going to cut school, and if he did, he certainly would not approve. Tom knew it. He couldn't risk being found out.

He'd get a whipping for sure. He listened as his brother's footsteps faded on the sidewalk in front of the house. They rented the small upstairs flat, which overlooked Black Bear Pass and the peaks of Telluride. It was a quick slide down the banister, a skip into the kitchen to grab his lunch on the table, and a leap off the back stoop onto the garden path. Danny lived a few blocks up the road in a modest two-story Queen Anne home, a signature style of building in the boon towns of Colorado.

Tom hated the walk past the Beaumont Hotel, the quickest way to Danny's house. Dark shadows from the towering gables spilled onto the road as though searching for young boys who had defiled the building's beauty. Guilt crept into his heart when he looked at the spot where he'd scratched his initials on the stone and brick wall of the gothic-styled structure on a double dare. There was no erasing his past sin. He had tried and now carried a scar on his forefinger as an everyday reminder that stone is stronger than a butter knife.

Tom touched the smooth cornerstone of the building with his pinky finger three times for luck. That chiseled-in date, 1898, was filled with magic—powerful black magic, according to his friend, Danny. For his mother, it meant a chance to tell her story to anyone who would listen *every* time she walked by the building. He thought about the first time he could remember that she told it.

> "One day, when I was a young girl about your age, Tom, my father took me to the train station in Grand Junction to pick up supplies. I watched a mule train pull next to the tracks, and men loaded wagon after wagon with leather chairs, carved tables and headboards, oriental rugs, and boxes of

crystal and china. Word spread that all these fine things had come from Chicago and were headed to Ouray, to this very hotel."

Archie, who was standing next to his wife, chimed in. "When they finished building the hotel, people came from *everywhere* for the grand opening. Dignitaries, cowboys, miners . . ."

"Even sweethearts," Trudi replied as she put her arms around Archie. She liked to see her boys squirm at the thought of cootie-ridden girls.

"*Everyone* wanted to stay at the Beaumont," Archie said with a smile as he enjoyed the grimaces on his boys' faces.

"Right here in the heart of Ouray on Main Street and Third. The whole top floor hosted the most wonderful parties!" Trudi said. "It was all ballroom!"

Archie laughed. "When everyone got paid on Friday nights, it was more like the *brawl* room!"

Tom heard rumors at school and knew his father would tell him true. "Is it haunted?"

Archie stroked his chin for a moment, then pulled the boys closer and whispered, "The sheriff told me himself that a bride was murdered by her husband on their wedding night!" He looked around the lobby to make sure no one was listening.

"After midnight, if you're real quiet . . . you'll hear her scream!" he said as he squeezed the boys around their necks.

The amused bartender smiled but said nothing as the scared boys ran across the lobby floor and bounded out the door.

Tom always ran that block and the block where Saint Joseph's Miner's Hospital is located. The stately red brick building, run by the Sisters of Mercy, occupied a beautifully manicured lot. Shrubs hugged the foundation, and in warmer months blue columbine lined the sidewalk. Those were his mama's favorite flowers.

Even from a block away, Tom recognized the form of a man standing in front of a long, narrow window on the second floor of the hospital. His face was filthy from the mine. Tobacco spittle stained his beard. Blood seeped onto the snowy white dressing bound around his head. The injured man looked at Tom with dark, hollow eyes and collapsed—in the window, right in front of Tom!

Two white figures floated towards the spot where the man had stood. A hand grabbed the drapes, and in one instant, the miner was gone.

Ghosts! Those were ghosts, Tom thought. They'd come for the miner. He was sure of it! He could feel it in his bones. And before they could get him, Tom fled.

Together, Danny and Tom weren't afraid of no ghosts. Or if they were, they didn't show it.

The boys waited until they heard the school bell toll then started down the trail. The pine needles were soft underfoot as the two youngsters began the climb to the lake. A glance back toward town exposed a majestic scene with mountain peaks and massive pines surrounding the cedar shake and brick buildings. Golden rays of sunlight shimmered in the jagged folds of the snow-tipped mountaintops.

Glimpses of the trail leading to Bird Mine appeared directly across from where they stood "as straight as a bird's flight," Tom's mama told him. To the south, the winding Million Dollar Highway led to Silverton and Durango—aptly named for all the money

Butch Cassidy and the Sundance Kid stole and laundered in this neck of the woods.

The boys stopped to examine fresh markings on the side of a tree.

"What do you think, Tom? Is it a bear?" Danny asked. His eyes expressed fear and excitement at the possibility of seeing a grizzly.

Tom walked around the tree with his hand on his slingshot, in case a bear crouched on the other side.

"Nah," he said with the feigned authority of a tracker. "I think the deer are getting their racks. This one's head itched."

"Kinda like yours when you're thinking, huh?" Danny ribbed as he ran up the mountainside and out of Tom's grasp.

Beyond the boulder bridge, wedged within a small gorge, the boys saw the fort they built last year before the winter snows made it impossible for them to make the half-mile trek up here. The back portion of the sapling roof collapsed, probably from snow weight, although the scrub tree branch where they hung their clothes while swimming was still attached to the pine bark wall.

Everything seemed smaller, possibly because both boys had grown three inches since last summer. Danny grew up and out and outweighed Tom by twelve pounds. The creek feeding the swimming hole churned past their feet, deeper and faster than Tom remembered.

"C'mon, chicken!" Danny shouted as he tested the fallen branch spanning the stream. "It's safe," he said as he jumped up and down.

"Don't do that—" Tom warned, the sentence cut off by the sickening crack of wood splintering. A brief scream pierced the air, and Danny hit the water with his back.

Tom jumped into the water, lunging after his friend. "Danny! Danny!"

His hands grabbed air as his friend bounced his way downstream in the frigid winter melt. Danny's head grazed the rocks along the way. Tom's shoes filled with water. His steps were labored in the thigh-high stream.

"Danny, grab my hand!" Tom shouted. There was no response.

Both boys tumbled end over end over the six-foot waterfall into the pool below. Tom began to sink from the weight of his coat and shoes. The cold took his breath away and made his muscles rigid. He fought to break the surface.

"Danny!" He shouted as he gulped another gasp of air and dove for the lake bottom again. Bubbles breaking next to his ears confused his senses. He broke the surface again and again, spinning wildly, looking for any sign of his friend.

"Danny!" he shouted as he spotted his friend's still body at the shallow end of the cove.

He half ran, half swam toward his best friend. Danny's angelic face stared up at Tom. Tom gently pulled Danny's lifeless body onto shore and began to wail.

Trudi sat in the darkened room, grateful to be alone; her eyes were bloated, her head throbbing from tears of grief. How could she be so torn by emotion yet void of animation? All movement labored, if at all. Grateful her son survived, yet laden with guilt because he lived and Danny didn't. Her heart broke for Danny's parents, and yet what could she say to comfort them? Nothing.

The family's photo album lay heavy on her lap, as heavy as the memories of the past few weeks that crushed her heart. She mindlessly turned the pages. Piles of crumpled tissues surrounded the davenport.

Her wedding picture, faded with age, portrayed a young woman beaming with love as a bride should. She sighed and turned the page.

Her fingers caressed the faces of her two sons, Spike and Tom, pictured on the steps of the one-room schoolhouse at Bird Mine. How she worried about them up there—not while they lived in town! An uncontrollable sob shook through her body, and she wiped at a tear coursing down her cheek.

A newspaper clipping sat kattywonker on the following page. The irony of the headline brought a contorted smile to her swollen face:

PRAISES HIS WIFE AND DIES

"This Is a Good Cup of Coffee," He Remarked to Wife of Thirty Years – Funeral Will Be Held Tomorrow Afternoon.

Newspaper obit clipping; Greeley, CO

Daddy would have enjoyed the humor of his obituary, she thought as she tenderly placed the article back in the album for safekeeping.

Tucked between the last page and back cover was an elaborately scripted document. "Joined Together in Holy Matrimony" read the words above their names.

"It takes two to be married," she bitterly muttered under her breath.

Where was Archie when she needed him most? When they needed him? The boys needed a father; she needed a husband. She yearned for a place to put down roots, to call home.

She knew when he came home it would be the same empty promises she'd heard for years. *Not this time,* she vowed. *Nope . . . not this time.*

Her fingers played with the tiny tear in the middle of the wedding certificate. She closed her eyes and ripped it in half and then in quarters, over and over again until nothing remained but holy confetti.

———

"Mom, you okay?" was the timid question asked from the kitchen's doorway.

Trudi blinked and looked around, trying to get her bearings. She was curled in a fetal position at the end of the couch. The photo album was wedged between the seat cushions. Sunlight streamed through the front room window, heralding a new day.

"What time is it?" she asked while rubbing the life back into her numb arm. Her head pulsed with every heartbeat.

"Almost seven," Spike replied as he brought his mother a cup of coffee.

"Seven!" she shouted. "Where's your brother? Tom!"

Spike took a step back as Trudi ran from suitcase to box, throwing last-minute items into the containers. "We've got fifteen minutes to be out the door."

"I don't want to move to Oregon," Tom stated defiantly as he stood behind his brother.

"And I don't want gray hair, but that's just the way it is, so get the rest of your belongings together—now, young man. You'll love Uncle Harry and Aunt Edith."

"What about Dad?"

"I left him a note," Trudi said as she turned the key in the lock one last time. The hastily scribbled message pinned to the kitchen table under her half-full coffee cup read:

> *Archie,*
> *An empty house is the price of a fool's gold!*
> *It's over.*
> *Trudi*

CHAPTER 8

1934

A Hand Up

The family sang loud and off key as Trudi set the cake in front of Tom. "Happy birthday to you!" ended in a crescendo.

Edith, Trudi's older sister, was happiest fussing in her kitchen. It was the gathering place for all meals, except holidays and birthdays when the dining room took on a festive air dressed in fine, white linens and bone china.

"I want a BIG piece," Babe announced to her aunt as she passed her plate. The nine year old loved chocolate and coconut as much as her brother.

"Twenty-two years old!" Uncle Harry said and shook his head as he pushed his pudgy frame away from the table. "I remember when you first came here as a little whippersnapper, Tom—cute as you could be!"

"Harry, you're embarrassing the lad," Edith scolded with a smile and a wag of her finger.

"That's my job," he replied as he slapped Tom on the back. "What else is an uncle to do, eh? Except say, I'm mighty proud of you, son. Helping your mama and baby sister the way you have. Today you're twenty-two. A full year of manhood, according to the law, but in reality, you've been a man for the last four years, since Spike's accident and the death of your step-daddy."

Edith snapped the back of Harry's neck with her finger as she shushed him.

"Ouch," he cried and swatted at her hand.

Tom glanced toward his mother as he blew out the candles.

"It's okay," Trudi said. "You don't have to walk on eggshells. Charles was a wonderful man, and I'm grateful for the five short years we had together. Look at the beautiful gift he gave me," she said as she kissed her little girl on the top of her head.

She paused for a moment, not noticing her sister glaring at her husband. "I'm even more grateful that you took us in—again! I don't know what I'd do without you!" she sobbed, choking back tears.

"Honey, you're welcome to stay with us as many times as you need and for as long as you like," Edith promised her sister with a hug around her shoulders.

"You can stay as long as you laugh at my jokes," Harry added.

Babe slid from her chair and walked toward Tom.

"We got you something," she announced as she carried a small box to his side of the table.

"Ma, you shouldn't have!" Tom said as he opened the package carefully and tenderly looked at the object. "This is Grandpa Adam's pocket watch. I remember him using it when I was a kid. I loved the Tinker's Wagon etched on the face."

"Look," he said as he showed it to his little sister, "the eyes of the donkey dart back and forth, counting the seconds. See? One . . . two . . . three . . ."

Trudi smiled. "I was waiting for just the right moment to give it to you, Tommy. Grandpa Adam's father gave it to him the day he left Scotland for America. Tomorrow, you're leaving home for the first time. Every time you look at that watch, remember you can do anything you set your mind to do. And as Grandpa Weir used to say, 'The results are all in God's time.'"

"Thanks, Ma. Thanks everybody. It's been a swell party!"

"Mama? Can I go outside?" Babe asked, wiping the last remnants of cake from her mouth.

"I'll take her, Ma," Tom said as Edith began clearing the table.

"You two go ahead," Trudi replied. "I'll be in the kitchen with Edith. Let me help you with that, dear!" she called after her sister.

Soap bubbles filled the sink and the teapot simmered on the stove, ready to rinse the dishes. Edith meticulously scrubbed first the glasses, then the plates, followed by the silverware, and only then the pots and pans.

"That was a wonderful meal," Trudi said as she picked up a frayed, hand-embroidered dish towel, a cherished and often-used gift from their mother. All three sisters received a pair of monogrammed towels in their favorite colors when they got married.

"I'm going to miss that boy of yours," Edith said.

"I know, but you still have Babe and me to torture you," Trudi replied as she gave her older sister a flick of the towel on her backside.

"Ow!" Edith cried and splashed dishwater on the front of Trudi's apron.

The girls began to laugh. "Did you hear that?" Trudi asked.

"What? I didn't hear anything."

"I thought I heard Mom tell us to behave or we'd do dishes the rest of our lives."

"Thirty years later, and what are we doing?" Edith questioned as she held her hands up, water dripping off her elbows. "Oh, Trudi, look at that beautiful sunset," Edith remarked as she looked out the window and across the valley.

Tom and Babe watched the sunset from the farmhouse porch as it slipped behind the mountain peaks and bathed the sky in red and purple and gold. "Do you know what they say when the sunset's this splendid?" Tom asked his little sister.

"Yeah, red skies at night, sailor's delight," She answered hesitantly. "What does that mean?" Her tiny hand petted Vino's head. The old collie nuzzled her for more.

"It means tomorrow's going to be another beautiful day."

"I don't think so," Babe said.

"Why do you say that?" Tom asked, surprised by her response.

"Because my heart feels gloomy . . . like rain. First Daddy dies. Then Spike gets hurt. And now you're leaving." Tears welled, and she buried her head in the dog's soft fur.

Tom cradled his baby sister. "I'm not going to be far away. In fact, I'll be at Crater Lake," Tom said. "We went camping there last summer, remember?"

"Are you going camping?"

"No. Well, sort of—but I'll be working, too. Have you heard of the Conservation Corps?"

"Bobby Noonan's dad calls it the Tree Army."

"It's more than that. You've seen pictures in the paper of people standing in line waiting for food, haven't you?"

"Yeah."

"That's because there aren't many jobs, and people need to work in order to eat. Well . . . President Roosevelt had a bright idea. He calls it The New Deal. He's asked three hundred thousand men to help improve our country, and we said yes."

"What are you going to do?"

"We're going to plant trees, but we're also building cabins and roads and bridges throughout our national forests."

"What happens if there's a forest fire?"

"We'll fight it."

"Will you meet the president?"

Tom laughed as he said, "No."

"Will Mrs. Roosevelt be there?"

"No. But if she is, I'll tell her you said hi."

"I like her! Mom says she has gumption." She looked at her brother and asked, "What's *gumption*?"

Tom laughed as he looked at his new pocket watch. "It's past your bedtime, cupcake. We'll look *gumption* up in the dictionary in the morning."

Babe danced under Uncle Harry's arm as he opened the screen door. He let out a sigh and lowered himself onto the stoop.

"Spent too much time squatting over grapevines today. I think we're going to have a record crop this year, if the weather holds out," the old man said while he rubbed his knees.

"That's good, Uncle Harry. I wish I could be here to help."

Harry shook his head. "Don't give it another thought. This Conservation Corps work is important. Besides, the twenty-five dollars sent to your mother every month will help her pay the rent in San Diego when she can afford to go. It's up to twenty dollars a month. Can you imagine? It's not like living here in Grant's Pass. To make matters worse, gas stations are asking ten cents for a gallon of gas! What's this world coming to? Between you, me, and Aunt Edith, we'll get Trudi through

Archie "Spike" Elliott,
18 years old

this mess. She needs to be with your brother."

Tom lit a cigarette and took a long drag. "Ma told me Spike's doing better. He's starting to walk again."

"Damn shame what happened. He had such a promising career as a boxer in the navy. If that piece of puke wanted to go AWOL, he should have just walked off base. No reason to knife Spike in the back and leave him for dead. He's gone through three years of hell stuck in that hospital bed."

The two men sat in silence. "Say, Tommy, I want to thank you for laying that narrow-gauge track around the vineyard. It's going to make my job a whole lot easier."

"Take it easy near the bridge," Tom warned. "The shale keeps shifting and may need to be shored up."

The men turned to look when the screen door hinge creaked.

"Hey, come join us, Ma."

"Oh that door sounds like my old bones," Harry said as he struggled to get up.

"Don't leave on my account," Trudi responded, easing onto the porch swing.

"No. I need to put some liniment on my joints and go to bed. Good night, you two," he said as he shuffled into the house. "Edith, where's that stinky salve?"

The world went silent, except for the hoots of an owl in the old oak next to the barn.

"This is my favorite time of day," Trudi said. "Look at all those stars . . . and the moon!"

A Hand Up

Tom couldn't sleep. He stared at the wooden floor in the eight-man tent and shivered. His breath came in short bursts of mist. It was the end of July. The camp, three miles from the ranger's station on eight thousand-foot Mount Mazama, near Medford, Oregon, had received a light coat of snow overnight.

It was 5:30 a.m. The smell of bacon drifted on the breeze as mess stewards prepared breakfast for the two hundred plus civilian conservation corpsmen in the encampment. Tom quietly slipped his trousers over his skivvies, grabbed his toilet kit and towel, and tiptoed to the privy and then to the creek to shave. It wouldn't be long before reveille sounded at Camp Wineglass NP-2 Company 1634.

"Elliott! You're wanted in the office," the young messenger shouted from the Model T as he chugged down the dirt trail, leaving tracks in the quickly melting snow.

"Thanks, Mike," Tom shouted back as he started his flatbed truck. Traces of limestone powder covered the planks from yesterday's haul. More stone and seedlings would be loaded this morning and lugged up the mountain to finish the retaining wall near the lodge. A couple of baking powder biscuits wrapped in a napkin sat on top of his sketch pad in the front seat.

Tom slowly opened the front door of the administration building. Mr. Ticknor motioned to the young enlistee with a nod of his head. "He's been waiting for you."

"Shut the door, son," Captain Merrill said as he straightened the papers on his desk.

"Yes, sir."

"I see you've been driving truck for us."

"Yes, sir."

"You like driving?"

"Yes, sir."

"No absences," he mumbled under his breath with a look of approval. "That's good." Merrill made a note in the margin of his papers.

The captain looked Tom in the eye with the piercing stare of a career military officer inspecting his troops. "I'm giving you a good report for your three months service with us," he said. "You're reliable and trustworthy—both excellent traits."

"Thank you, sir."

"But take this advice to heart: finish your schooling. If you were staying with the corps, I'd encourage you to take the night classes we offer. One year of high school is not enough. Someday, you'll be married with a family of your own. You owe it to them and to yourself to finish your education."

"Yes, sir," Tom said quietly as he stared at his feet. *What does he mean if I stay with the corps?* Tom wondered.

"Ticknor!" the captain called out. "Is that letter ready?"

"Yes, sir," the supervisor responded and handed the envelope to Tom. "You'll need this."

"Am I being fired?" Tom asked, not sure he wanted to hear the answer. His jaw tightened in anticipation of bad news.

"Hell no!" Captain Merrill replied. "Do you remember applying for a job at a trucking firm in California last March?"

"Yes, sir."

"They're giving you a job. You start next Monday."

Tom let out a whoop and shook Captain Merrill's hand like he was priming a well for water.

"Thank you, sir!"

"You can use the phone on my desk to call your family," Ticknor offered.

"Thank you, sir!"

A Hand Up

"Number, please?" asked the operator.

He listened to the multiple bursts of tone assigned to the vineyard house and wondered if nosey Mrs. Cullom at the farm down the road would pick up the party line.

Tom heard Edith's wispy voice answer, "Hello?"

"I have a collect call from a Tom Elliott. Will you accept the charges?"

Edith's gasp was audible. "Of course we will!" She hollered as she held the phone out at arm's length, "Trudi! Tommy's on the telephone!"

His mother's footsteps on the kitchen's linoleum echoed like a Vaudeville soft-shoe act. "Is he okay?" Trudi asked Edith before picking up the phone.

Breathlessly, Trudi asked, "Tommy, are you okay?"

"Yeah . . . I'm fine, Ma. Come and get me."

"What did you do?!"

"Nothing, Ma. Pack everything up and come get me. That trucking job in California came through. I have to be there next Monday. Can we do that?"

Tom with borrowed truck

"Harry!" Trudi yelled. "Come here! Tommy's on the telephone."

Tom could hear the old man shuffling across the floor. "Is he okay?"

"Tommy, you okay?" Harry asked.

"I'm fine, Uncle Harry. I got the job! I have to be in California next Monday. Can you help us?"

"I'll talk to Mr. Cox and see if we can borrow one of his trucks. Either way, we'll see you tomorrow, son."

The smell of pine in rarified air reminded Tom of his boyhood campouts with his brother and father in Colorado. Oh, the stories they spun 'round the fire pit at night about Injuns and bears and gold while eating Empson beans straight from the can. He learned to skip stones at Island Lake. The Rockies were magnificent, barefaced rocks which erupted from the plains thousands of years ago when tectonic plates shifted beneath the earth's surface. In contrast, the Cascades, a younger mountain range, formed when volcanic eruptions and violent implosions occurred. They paled in comparison to the size of the Rockies, although majestic in their own right.

Tom stood on the 1,800-foot caldera wall rim surrounding Crater Lake. Like a well-polished mirror, the sapphire-blue waters below reflected heaven and nature in all its beauty. He was awestruck by the free-formed sculptings created when molten lava spewed and cooled on the sheer walls of the bowl-shaped lake. Outcroppings with ominous names like Devil's Spine, Pumice Castle, Phantom Ship, and Wizard Island brought visitors face to face with the Master's work of Creation.

He flipped open the top on Uncle Harry's Brownie camera and sheltered the lens from the intense sunlight with his hand.

A Hand Up

Someday, someone will invent a color camera the average Joe can afford, he thought, but for now he'd have to commit to memory the translucent colors of turquoise, green, and gold that hugged the shoreline.

"Uncle Harry, would you mind stopping at the entrance station on our way out? My friend Ernie's on duty today, and I want to say good-bye."

"Sure thing, Tommy."

The Model T truck, filled with all the family's worldly possessions, chugged and sputtered down the road toward the guard shack.

"Yowza!" Uncle Harry exclaimed.

"Look at that touring car coming into the park. Bet that cost more than a buck two eighty!"

Ernie stood board stiff at the guard entrance as he talked to the two women in the automobile.

"That looks like Mrs. Roosevelt," Trudi said as she craned to see who was in the car.

"It *is* Mrs. Roosevelt!" Babe shouted. The nine year old jumped out of the truck and ran after her brother, mindful that he promised to introduce her to the first lady if they ever met.

Tommy stopped motionless behind Ernie and stared at Mrs. Roosevelt. His voice crackled like a twelve year old as he said, "It's an honor to meet you. Babe . . ."

Surprise and shock shrouded Mrs. Roosevelt's face! Her head whipped around, and she stared straight ahead as she and her secretary sped off. Babe held her brother's hand and waved wildly after the quickly disappearing auto.

"Did you meet her?" Trudi asked as the two piled back in the truck burgeoning with household goods.

Tom's face flushed with embarrassment.

"You've got to come up with another nickname for Ethelyn, Ma," he said, shaking his head.

"Why?"

"Because the first lady of the United States thinks I just called *her* Babe!"

CHAPTER 9

1935

Love, Honor, and Obey

Arthur Hampton held the powdered dirt in his hand and watched it sift through his fingers. The wind carried the dust toward the road in drifting circles. It was a wicked weather day today—even more so than yesterday or the day before that . . . or last spring. Six-foot drifts of sandy soil piled against the two-story clapboard building. Five years of drought in the parched Nebraska Plains had taken its toll on the farm and family: his three beautiful daughters as bare of adornment as the house itself.

"I'm not backing down," he muttered under his breath as he thought back to last night's argument. Easily confused by feminine logic and driven by fatherly love, he did not understand her anger at him. It sparked like the static electricity dancing across the barbed-wire fences during a dust storm. Didn't she realize that he had no choice! It was his obligation to protect her.

Elizabeth missed living near her sisters when all three families were blocks away from each other in Colorado. It just wasn't the same writing to the other two now that they lived in Oregon and she in Nebraska. The sound of their voices calmed her in times of trouble, and right now she needed that.

My Dear Sisters,
The dust storms continue to destroy everything in sight. We pray for rain. Lillian has been smitten by the likes of a stranger. She and her father are at odds over love.

The door flew open. Elizabeth dropped her pen and quickly slipped the partially written note into the desk drawer.

"I'm sixteen years old, Daddy—practically a grown woman!" Lillian pouted. Tears streamed down her face.

"Watch how you talk to your father," her mother cautioned. "You have no mind to sass."

"But, Mama, I love him!"

"Love?" Arthur boomed. "What do you know about love? What do you know about this man? He's a drifter. A no good drifter that blew into town on the wind, and as soon as he has his way with you, he'll blow right on out of here. I know his kind, Lillian, and you are to have nothing to do with him. Do you understand?"

Lillian let out a high-pitched groan.

"That's enough, child," her mother said as she tried to put her arm around the heartbroken girl to comfort her.

Lillian's younger sister, awakened by the uproar, beckoned the sobbing girl to the loft, where their cots faced each other on the far end of the open space.

"Here, you sit here, honey," Helen said as she straightened the quilted coverlet on her sister's bed.

"What are you going to do?" she asked as she stroked Lillian's trembling hand.

"I don't know," the broken-hearted young woman sniffled.

Their mother brought them a cup of tea with a spot of honey. "This and a good night's sleep will calm your nerves. We'll talk in the morning."

The incessant howl of the wind brought a fine spray of powdered dust into the sparsely decorated home. It had happened every night for years. Scorpion trails skittered across the floorboards. By morning, shoes needed to be shaken before worn, unless you wanted a nasty sting. All types of creatures sought shelter from the Black Blizzards. Centipedes burrowed into the remnants of wallpaper. Spiders hid in cabinets, and scorpions hid under rag rugs. Nothing was sacred!

Friday morning began with the ritualistic sound of coughing. Dust was everywhere: in the nose and eyes; around the teeth; and in the lungs. Wet rags placed over their faces before going to sleep were dry by morning. All were developing a terrible cough and worried it may be the start of dust pneumonia.

"Mama!" Helen screamed between coughs. "Lillian's gone!" She heard her father's feet hit the floor.

He shook the dust and critters away from his shoes, "Where did she go?" he shouted.

"What, Papa?" Helen responded, hoping to bide some time to gather her thoughts.

"Your father asked you, 'Where did she go?'" her mother shouted as she climbed to the loft. "This is no time to play coy!"

The relentless wind howled outside.

Lillian pulled her scarf over her mouth and nose. Even with her head bowed, the dust stung her eyes as she slogged down the road. It was dangerous walking the half-mile to town in the light of day, much less before dawn. Wild animals foraged for food. A neighbor told her family that an eight-mile roundup in Oklahoma last month netted thirty-five thousand black-tailed jackrabbits.

Hard to imagine, she thought. She quickened her step and thought about the love of her life. She and Edgar were about to marry this morning at the Colby homestead on the outskirts of town. She didn't dare tell her sister. Helen would have told their mother, and Mother . . . well, she would have told their father.

The next time she saw her family, she'd be Mrs. Edgar Fiscus. And that would be that!

Arthur sat in the sheriff's office, righteous anger and fatherly fear clouding his thoughts and features.

"Charlie, this guy is no good!"

"We find him . . . we'll find her," the sheriff confidently responded without looking up from his desk. "I've got a deputy down at the boarding house checking on him right now," he said as he poured another cup of coffee. "You want some?" the lawman asked, holding the percolator towards Arthur.

Arthur rubbed his arthritic hands and shook his head no. The pain in his fingers was nothing compared to the pain in his heart.

"He'll be back any minute. In the meantime, I'm looking for a message from my friend at the newspaper in Omaha to see what he found out about this guy."

"Thanks, Charlie."

The sheriff placed his hand on Arthur's shoulder. "As one dad to another, we'll find her. And if he's dirty . . . we'll get him."

Lillian beamed as she heard the circuit preacher say, "I now pronounce you husband and wife." A pang of sadness gripped her. If only her family shared her joy. Edgar bent over, picked her up, and carried her out the door and up the street.

"I have a surprise for you, Mrs. Fiscus."

He heard her giggle from under the hanky she held in front of her face.

"Mrs. . . . I am Mrs. Fiscus!" She nuzzled his neck as he carried his bride up the steps of the Grand Hotel.

Sheriff Charlie Carter studied the telegraph in his hand. His jaw flexed at the news. "Come on, Art," he said as he strapped on his holster.

Lillian sat on the edge of the bed, now knowing the full beauty of being a woman. She looked at her husband, sleeping peacefully, and bent over to kiss him when there was a pounding of fists on the door.

"Open up! We know you're in there!" shouted the sheriff and his deputy.

Lillian screamed and pulled the covers around her naked body at the sound of the key in the lock. The door flew open! Disoriented, Edgar rolled to the floor. His leg caught in the bedding. A flash from the reporter's camera captured the moment: the only wedding photo of Mr. and Mrs. Fiscus, except for Edgar's mug shot.

"Edgar Fiscus, you are under arrest!" shouted the sheriff.

The morning headline read:

POLYGAMY LAW EXACTS PENALTY AT ROMANCE END

Edgar A. Fiscus, Husband of Aurora Girl, Admits Truth of Father-in-Law's Accusation: First Wife in Nebraska

CHAPTER 10

1936

Coast to Coast

Spike curled the hook of his cane around the side-view mirror on the truck and hoisted himself into the cab of the eighteen-wheeler.

"You need anything before we take off?" Tom asked as he watched his brother struggle to get comfortable. It was a miracle he was able to walk at all.

"I'll take a cup a mud for the road," he said. "Two sugars and a cloud of cream."

The little diner tucked into the Redwoods next to dead man's curve near the sleepy town of Skunk Hollow was a favorite with truckers on Highway One-O-One. The coffee poured strong and steamy, the waitresses steamier.

It was the end of the summer logging harvest and Tom's last haul before moving to San Diego. He checked the rigging and marveled at the natural beauty of the eight-ton cedars he transported to the mill.

Spike patiently waited for his brother. He looked forward to this ride. It was his first outing since the stabbing four years ago, unless you counted doctor appointments and physical therapy.

"What happens when these things get to the mill?" Spike asked.

"Each log's lifted by a giant boom," Tom shouted above the road noise as he downshifted for a hairpin turn. "Then they're rolled onto a conveyor. The shimmy action breaks off all remaining scrub limbs."

"The noise must be deafening," Spike hollered above the rumble of the truck's engine.

"It's quiet as a nursery compared to the next room," Tom said with a wink. "There's a buzz saw—larger than a man! It squares off each side, exposing the green wood under the bark," Tom said while his hand demonstrated the action.

It was difficult to tell which made more noise, the truck's compression air brakes or the music blaring from the radio. Spike pulled two cigarettes from his shirt pocket, tapped the loose tobacco on the side of the rig, lit them, and passed one to his brother.

"Once the boards are cut and dried in kilns," Tom said after he exhaled, "the pieces are processed and separated according to their quality. Some are destined for construction, others for furniture. Even wood chips are saved. Nothing's wasted."

Spike shifted in his seat and gingerly clutched his neck. A groan escaped with a sigh when runaway spasms sent bolts of pain throughout his body.

"You okay?" Tom asked.

"Yeah . . ."

Tom wondered how Spike would do on the narrow, gravel road alongside the train tracks at the mill. Even at low speeds, the rig shimmied and swayed on rough patches. Jostling would be inevitable. *No sense worrying about it now*, he thought as he took another drag on his cigarette. He'd figure it out when he got there.

Shadows dappled the highway, and the noise from the big rig startled the occasional hawk searching for a morning meal. The road became a never-ending loop of trees broken by a handful of one-room log cabins clustered under oversized NO v-a-c-a-n-c-y signs.

They rolled through old-stand timber in northern California until the forest met the ocean. Tom pulled over just south of Eureka on the skirt of a crescent-shaped beach mounded with sand dunes and littered with driftwood. Twenty-foot waves rolled and crashed on the boulders off shore, sending a fine sea-salt mist into the air.

"We're almost there," Tom said as Spike rubbed the side of his neck.

"Take your time," Spike responded. He blew on his coffee and slurped a mouthful.

He slowly turned his head from side to side, capturing the moment. Plumes of sea oats gently swayed on the dunes. Wave foam laced the beach and disappeared as the next wave washed over it. Tiny birds darted along the water's edge. The ocean and sky blended into one mottled shade of blue.

He put his good arm behind his head and rested his leg on the dash. The furrows of pain upon his face visibly softened.

"I forgot how large and beautiful the world really is."

Meanwhile in Colorado, Archie balanced on the back two legs of the rickety chair just like his daddy used to do: arms folded over his belly, chin resting on his chest. Each inhaled breath saturated with the smell of hot metal, grease, dust, and steam. A distant and decisive ker-chunk of a locomotive coupling with its rolling stock near the loading docks jolted him awake. He cast a sideward glance down the railway station's platform to see if anyone caught him napping. One lone figure walked toward him.

"The Interurban's late again," the general freight agent, Mr. Robbins, growled. He rested his foot on the edge of a luggage cart parked next to Archie's chair. Robbins shook his head and muttered, "Second time this week! They've had trouble with the water tank ten miles down the line."

"How much water does that tank hold?" Archie asked.

"Fifty thousand gallons," Robbins responded. "But that's not the problem. It's a gravity-fed system. There's a point where the gooseneck spout just quits. Maintenance has been down there all day."

Archie looked at his watch, then down the track west towards Fruita.

"It better get here soon," Robbins said. "The train from Denver arrives at six."

Archie leaned forward when he saw his brother, Murray, push through the massive oak doors from the lobby of the two-story depot.

"What brings you here?" Robbins asked.

"We're waiting for a telegraph about a shipment of pig iron. We got the contract to manufacture the manhole covers for the city of Grand Junction."

Manhole cover made by Western Slope Foundry

Robbins shook his head and laughed. "Archie, only the Western Slope Foundry could turn sewage into gold."

"I just saw John and Jim from the Fruit Growers Association," Murray said as he joined the two men. "They estimate they'll ship three hundred freight cars of apples this fall."

"I don't think it's all going to market by train," said Robbins. "Trucks eat into our profits every day now that roads are improving."

"Nothing stays the same," Murray replied with a cluck of his tongue.

Archie's gaze wandered past the eight-stall roundhouse and turntable to the rolling hills and mesas beyond. "When we moved here in 1902, this was a little frontier town with dirt roads."

"Ten years before that," Robbins added, "when I came here, Chief Ouray and the Ute nation occupied this land all the way to the San Juan mountains. Those were tense times between the white man and the tribes."

Archie reached into his back pocket for a tin of snuff.

"Kit Carson helped convince Chief Ouray to settle on the reservation in Utah, but still, rumors of braves coming into Grand Junction from time to time set fear in the hearts of our women and children."

"You were pretty young back then," Archie said to his brother. "The Denver and Rio Grande Depot wasn't even a pencil mark from the hand of Henry Schlack."

"Now this station is the pride of Grand Junction," Robbins boasted.

The three men stared at the two-story, limestone building with the arched windows and Tuscan columns. The red terra-cotta roof could be seen for miles in any direction, and when the sun was on the horizon, the color dazzled like a cut ruby against the blue sky.

"It's a showstopper!" Murray whistled under his breath.

"This depot welcomes travelers from every corner of the globe," Robbins said with pride.

"I remember father telling me that this depot links people and commerce from border to border and coast to coast," added Archie.

"This depot caused a boon in population and economic growth across our nation," said Robbins with a wave of his hand. "Your daddy used to call Grand Junction the gateway to the world."

"It's certainly been good to us and the foundry," Murray added as he looked at his watch.

"Do you remember when the depot had its official opening?" Archie asked.

"It was 1906," Murray answered with certainty. "Twelve days before the San Francisco earthquake."

"Now that's a day I'll never forget! I was sixteen," Murray added. "I'd hang around the station, waiting for the telegraph operator to either send or receive a message. I was fascinated by the clatter of Morse code. But that day I watched the operator's face turn ashen as he copied the message."

"I remember Mrs. Price organizing the women in town. They collected clothing for the refugees," said Robbins. "Some of the people rode the train from San Francisco to here in nothing but their nightclothes. That's all they had!"

Archie shook his head, thinking of the horror these passengers experienced, when a car horn startled the men. They looked toward the road in time to see a horse cart dart across the road.

A smile crossed Archie's face as he glanced at the corner of the building where luggage piled up until the trains arrived. He thought of a stolen kiss between him and Trudi on a beautiful, moonlit evening, so long ago. This memory he held close in his heart and intended to keep it locked within. It had been twelve years since she left and took the kids. Oh, how he missed his family.

His boys were young men now, possibly with families of their own. He hadn't heard from them since the California Zephyr left this station. The *what-ifs* tensed his body as the anger and remorse briefly rose to the surface. Yet, how could he hate his wife? He created the events that drove her away.

Archie jumped from the jab to his arm. "Ten years later," Robbins continued with their reminiscences, now that he had Archie's attention, "Mesa County recruits, including your brother, Walter, left on troop transports from this very station to fight the Great War in France."

"Corporal Weir returned home a hero for his bravery in the battles at Saint Mihiel and the Argonne Forest," said Murray with a puff of pride for his brother. "He told me the eighteen months of service didn't hold a candle to General Pershing's regiment of 3,500 Yanks marching in the victory parades of Paris, London, New York, and Washington, D.C. All those women throwing kisses . . ."

"And lacies," Archie added with a laugh.

"Did you know he met the king of England and the king of Belgium?" Murray added.

"I read about it in the papers," Robbins replied.

"Lookie there!" Archie said as passengers began to line up.

Robbins disappeared into the crowd shouting, "Have your tickets ready! Tickets, please."

In the distance, a thin wisp of smoke and steam curled skyward.

"I'm going to check on that telegraph," Murray said as he pushed his chair back against the wall.

Archie looked toward the mountains with an ache in his heart. He interlocked his fingers across his belly and rested his chin upon his chest . . . just like his father used to do.

Swedish Connection

BEGOTTEN: With Love

CHAPTER 11

1892

Amerika

The eighteen year old laughed as he pounded the side of the table with his mug, demanding more whiskey. His shirt, stained with sweat and puke, clung to him as testimony that this was not his first drink tonight, although he silently vowed it would be his last. The room spun and objects blurred as he looked in the direction of the nearly empty bottle. He closed his eyes and prayed the waves of nausea would stop.

Uncontrolled spasms of pain in his right side dropped him to his knees and he fell, curled in a fetal position, near the edge of the open hearth. The intense heat of the flames on the bare skin of his neck warned him to roll no farther. John's plaintive moans pierced the heart of Anders as the stoutly man hooked his hands under his son's arms and pulled him away from harm. John, barely conscious, slowly recoiled from the smoldering ember burning the palm of his hand.

"Get up, son," the somber-faced Anders said firmly as he propped John on the long bench next to the kitchen door.

"I can't do this, Dad," John's hoarse voice rasped. His face flushed with fever and pain.

"If you don't, you'll die!" Anders said as he cradled his firstborn in his arms. He held the bottle to John's lips until the young man guzzled another swig.

The farmhouse door burst open with a blast of arctic air. Swirls of snow dropped to the floor with every booted step the imposing figure took. He barked orders over his shoulder to the shadowy figures in the courtyard. One silent command from a mounted Dragoneer and the entourage of wagons and horsemen disappeared in the falling snow.

Nils quickly latched the door, pulled a chair next to his grandson, and straddled the seat. His massive arms rested on the wooden back. The smell of wet wool, horse sweat, and leather caused John to heave into the blanket on his lap. The old man sighed and rested his chin on his hands. The assessment of his progeny was grim.

"He needs surgery, now," Nils said to Anders in his slow, Skåne drawl, distinctive to the southern regions of Sweden.

Anders nodded his head in resignation. There were no trains running to Malmö or Lund or Christianstad in this storm. Even if there were, his child was too ill to be moved. If John's appendix burst before they operated, the boy would surely die.

"I've sent Anna and the children to Bjärsjölagård," Anders said as he stroked the hair of his unconscious son.

"Their sleigh arrived as I was leaving," Nils replied. "Anna's mother will know what to do to comfort them."

Nils poured another glass of whiskey. His gnarled hand held it steady as he pushed it toward the sleeping lad. "Wake him up."

Even at midmorning, the skies were barely light. The weather was eerily silent after two days of blizzard. Nils and Anders carried the boy from the farmhouse to the hastily erected field hospital before the clouds cleared and the temperature dropped.

Lights flickered in the operating room as medics from the first battalion prepared for surgery. A fresh bottle of whiskey was set next to the surgical instruments. Ligatures to secure John's limbs were tethered to the table; and a leather strap for his mouth, so his teeth didn't break when he clenched from the pain, occupied the far end of the instrument tray. All was ready for the unsuspecting patient.

"John, wake up!" Lars shouted with excitement as he gave the eighteen year old a rough shake to the shoulder. "We're here!"

John opened his eyes, too tired to move. His back was stiff from sleeping in the canvas hammock; his side was still tender from the surgery nine months earlier, even though you could barely see a scar. His hands were raw from peeling potatoes for 311 passengers for the past three weeks to pay his passage to Amerika.

He no longer heard the rhythmic chug of the vessel's steam engines nor felt the roll of the waves. All was still and quiet in the Behren Island Narrows, where the ship transporting the immigrants from Scandinavia dropped anchor.

"Amerika!" A smile broke out on his face.

The passengers clustered around the ladder, waiting for the hatch to open. There were no windows in steerage. No ventilation. And no relief from the weeks of stench and misery caused by rough weather and close quarters. The vast darkness punctuated only by three oil lamps cast sharp shadows on the men, magnifying their gaunt features.

"Amerika," John said softly under his breath. The smile broke into a grin.

The hatch opened and sunlight blazed through the tiny hole. Men winced and looked away, their eyes too sensitive after twenty-one days in the dark. John gathered his bed linens, satchel, coat, and hat.

"I'm coming as soon as I find my shoe," he said, not wanting to put his hands or bare foot on the decking. God only knows what he'd find.

A thin partition separated the men's quarters from the family sector in the midsection of the ship. The partitions didn't dampen the sound of seasick children nor the bleats of the livestock stowed forward with baggage and cargo.

"There's your shoe," Lars said, pointing with the tip of the artist brush he carried in his pocket.

It was impossible to stand straight in the hold for anyone over six feet tall. John's neck was cricked from stooping. He reached the hatch of the cargo hold and expelled the last breath of rancid, steerage air. The brush of sea breeze crossing his face as he walked toward the railing left him giddy.

He placed his fingers on the tattered leaflet in his pocket, the one he received from the Steamship Company two years prior: Come to America. Live Free. Follow your dreams in the land of opportunity. *The drawing on the cover didn't capture the enormity of the skyscrapers,* he thought as he held the page even with the horizon. The skyline of New York was more beautiful than he imagined!

Here he stood, poised to enter the gateway to his dreams. Yet, his thoughts raced to his family in Ahlestatorp, Sweden, and the tears and laughter of his farewell party. Friends from all over the district gathered in the family's stable for a night of feasting and dancing. The image of his mother standing in the doorway overlooking the rolling hills of their vast farmland haunted him, though. The warm glow of the lanterns softened the lines on her face and highlighted her high cheekbones (a family trait passed on from generation to generation). Her warm smile, which greeted him as he clasped her hand, couldn't conceal the sadness in her eyes.

"This will be the last time I see you while I'm still alive, my dear son," the old woman said as she wrapped her arm around her eldest son's waist.

He nodded and felt the lump grow in his throat.

"It's okay," Anna said reassuringly when she realized his discomfort. "This is meant to be."

John's gaze followed hers as she watched a carriage filled with revelers tether their horse to a tree.

"I will come here and remember all the happy times we've shared," Anna said. "No regrets. You have my love and blessing."

"Mama . . ." John stammered.

Anna placed her fingers to his lips. "Son, make this world a better place with that beautiful mind of yours. And when you have a family of your own, love them beyond measure, even if it means letting them be free to do what God intends them to do."

A wisp of a girl barely five feet tall broke through the crowd. "John!" shouted his younger sister, Caroline, breathlessly. "Your brothers are waiting for you to get into costume. Hurry!"

John, his five brothers, and two sisters were a fun-loving pod, he being the eldest. They'd become a popular favorite at parties as a ragtag mix of musicians. Their zany antics, music, and self-deprecating comedy were met with hoots and hollers.

"We never say no to a party, do we?" Anna shouted to Caroline above the crowd's cheers.

"Our family would celebrate the opening of a letter!" his sister shouted back.

John pulled a monogrammed hanky from his vest pocket, a gift from his sisters. The faint scent of vanilla and roses lingered within its folds. Anna taught the girls to crush flower petals and soak them in spices rather than frivolously spend a krona on expensive perfumes.

"John," Lars shouted as the young man quickly placed the hanky back in his pocket, "you stand here daydreaming much longer and the ship will sail back to Sweden with you still on it!"

Immigrants crowded onto the ferry. This was the final journey to Ellis Island, then to the golden streets of New York City and beyond. He and Lars climbed the steps to the top deck, breathing in the fresh harbor air. Seagulls circled overhead, waiting for any sign of a dropped morsel.

"What's today's date?" John asked his friend.

"August eighteenth," Lars answered as he pulled a flask from his coat pocket. "A new land . . . a fresh start," he said as he took a swig and held it out for John to do the same. "We have before us, John, a clean canvas."

John stood with his arms resting on the railing. "Arton," he said to his friend.

Lars looked at him oddly. "Ya," he answered hesitantly, waiting for his friend to finish his thought.

Unbeknownst to Lars, John and his siblings decided to break from tradition when they were all living at Ahlestatorp. In Sweden, if they took their father's name, (the patronymic system of assigning surnames in Scandinavia), their last name would have been Andersson—a fine name but overused, they all agreed. They wanted to stand out, to be remembered, because they had great plans for their futures. Yet, it was important to them to not forget from whence they came.

Their farm address was 17 Ahlestatorp. This land had been in the family for many generations, nearly a century, according to the property's lease. It was common sense then for the youngest generation to change their name to Arton, *eighteen* in Swedish. Arton. A symbolic moving from the home of their forefathers to their rightful place in the new world with all the possibilities it held for them.

"Arton," he reasoned, "a reminder of my heritage and the day I landed in Amerika." John felt this was an omen of good things to come.

He studied the ribbons of color in the harbor's water and quietly said, "It's important that my future children and grandchildren know this day changed the course of their history. A new land . . . a new name! From now on, my full name is John Leon Andersson Arton."

"Ahhh, the first stroke of color on your American canvas," Lars said with a wide swish of his paintbrush.

"I propose a toast," John said as he took the flask from his friend.

He held it toward the magnificent three hundred-foot statue standing tall on Bedloe's Island in the middle of the harbor. The folds of her copper garment mottled green with oxidation. Her left arm cradled the book of law close to her breast. Her right hand held high the torch, the symbol of hope and freedom. This beacon, covered with twenty-four-carat gold and emblazoned by kerosene lanterns, illuminated the harbor even in daylight. This awesome vision welcomed those yearning to reach the shores of a new nation and a life lived freely.

"Let's drink to the most beautiful woman in the world!" John said as he tipped the flask. "Here's to Miss Liberty!"

Lars pulled a small bottle from his inside coat pocket and added with a smile, "A toast to liberty and my *new* friend, John Arton."

BEGOTTEN: With Love

CHAPTER 12

1896

Indentured Servitude

"Oh my," Hedvig gasped aloud as she stared at the imposing three-story mansion. It had been a rainy carriage ride from Union Station in downtown Chicago to the *Castles of Hyde Park*, as the majestic estates were referred to by the locals. She was chilled to the bone.

"No need to stand out here," said the coachman as he picked up the satchel and opened the kitchen door for the young girl. "If you need anything, my name is Otto Pehrsson."

Three women cheerfully chatted in their native language as they prepared the evening meal in the newly remodeled kitchen. No longer did they cook over open fireplaces. Ingrid still carried the scars from the embers that caught her skirt on fire last year, a common hazard around open hearths. The expansive kitchen had: five cast-iron combination ranges with ventilated roll curtains; massive, walk-in iceboxes that hugged the exterior walls; and ceiling-to-floor cupboards and shelves with every kitchen utensil and cookbook imaginable lining the interior walls. Gaslights hung over the preparation tables in the middle of the room. Rumor had it these lights would be converted to electricity by the end of next year.

Hedvig couldn't help but stare at the well-stocked kitchen while the staff continued their chores. Two large, metal compartments contained a barrel worth of flour and sugar each and a wooden bin held twelve pounds of salt. These were situated near the six-foot-long wooden kneading table.

A young woman in a crisply ironed, floor-length apron kneaded a batch of dough. She deftly rounded the biscuits, lined them on a seasoned baking pan, and draped it with a dampened linen cloth so the mixture wouldn't dry out as it rose.

Otto reentered the kitchen with an armful of wood for the parlor fireplaces and stacked it in the far corner of the kitchen. The coach/footman used the cord of dried wood every morning to stoke the fireplaces in the mansion's parlors before the family rose.

"How do you do?" greeted the housekeeper after directing the staff in last-minute particulars for the evening's meal. She was a plain-looking woman, a head taller than the rest.

Hedvig met her gaze and responded with a slight nod of her head and a polite, "Mrs.," a title reserved for the second-in-command of the household, *the* representative of the mistress.

"Ingrid, please let Mrs. Langston know her latest charge arrived."

The jovial, ruddy complexioned woman took her leave up the servant's stairs hidden from view by the pantry in the back of the kitchen.

"I'm Karna Hanson," the housekeeper said as she made formal introductions. "The woman who just left is Ingrid Olson, the kitchen maid, and this is Kirsten Nilsson, our professed cook."

Hedvig responded slowly in her perfectly schooled English, "It's nice to meet you. I am Hedvig Svensson from Klinte, Gotland, Sweden."

Ingrid returned, out of breath. "Mrs. Langston asked that I take her to our room so she may freshen up. She will greet her after dinner at nine o'clock in her sitting parlor."

The two young women hesitated for a moment until Karna said, "Go! We have a meal to prepare."

Indentured Servitude

The tiny servants' quarter above the kitchen was clean and adequate. Six single beds lined two walls. There were two small bureaus and one washstand. A five-by-six-foot sitting room was attached at the far end (a luxury for servants) and an indoor, communal toilet was at the end of the hall.

"This is your bed. You don't want to sleep next to Karna," she cautioned. "She sings in her sleep!"

Hedvig laughed. She had shared a room with her three sisters back home. Only a thin sheet divided them from their four brothers.

"This is your bureau drawer. Your maid's uniform is hanging in the armoire we share . . . we share!" she repeated, making sure the newest girl understood that closet room was a precious commodity.

"Our meal is served at seven o'clock. You are expected to be there promptly," she added and then swiftly descended the stairs.

The rich timbre of the heirloom grandfather's clock reverberated through the halls of the family's private chamber. The brass clapper slowly struck nine in rhythm with the downswing of the pendulum.

Mrs. Langston looked over her spectacles at Hedvig and asked, "Do you understand what *indentured* means?"

"Yes, madam," Hedvig replied and recited it as taught in school: "It means I have committed to serve you for a period of five years. In return, you have paid my fare to America and will provide me room, board, and an allowance for personal needs. A portion of the allowance must be saved to repay you for my fare. If it is not repaid, then I must continue serving you until the debt is repaid in full."

Hedvig handed Mrs. Langston her letter of introduction from the head mistress at the Practical Household School in Stockholm for training maidservants.

"How old are you, Miss Svenson?" Mrs. Langston asked Hedvig. She felt a pang of motherly protection for this woman-child.

The young girl flushed and looked self-consciously at the floor. Her auburn hair, pinned up and away from her face, radiated in the gaslight. Confused, Hedvig wondered if she should have worn her street clothes instead of the uniform she found in the chest. The crisp, white blouse with puffy, leg-of-mutton sleeves and pinched waistline was large on her. The collar exposed the nape of Hedvig's neck, even though she clasped the onyx cameo as close to her throat as possible.

"I was seventeen in February," she said.

"I see," Mrs. Langston replied. She hesitated for what seemed an eternity. "In America, you are not considered emancipated until your eighteenth birthday. You will not be permitted to date until then. You are not to date any of the help in this household. You are to keep all matters of this household private. I expect you to be punctual and courteous. There is to be no cursing or vulgarities. Your duties will be: ladies maid and traveling companion to me and my daughter when she is with me. I want you to serve me when I entertain visitors on Thursday afternoons. Karna Hanson, our housekeeper, will direct you in the affairs of the kitchen. I understand you are trained as a pastry chef."

"Yes, madam," Hedvig replied.

"Then I want you to work closely with our professed cook on special occasions."

Hedvig responded with a short curtsey, her shoe inadvertently stepping on the floor-length skirt.

The lady of the house paused for a moment as she looked at Hedvig's hair. "I want to make this clear. Young women of breeding do not use cosmetics or hair dyes, and neither does my staff."

"This is my natural color," Hedvig replied as she bent her head closer to Mrs. Langston. The auburn highlights shone like copper throughout the blond tendrils.

"Do tell," the woman replied as she felt the soft, upswept bun. "Beginning tomorrow," Mrs. Langston continued, "you will be my travelling companion for the following month to familiarize yourself with the manners and protocol of America. Meet me in the parlor at eight o'clock sharp. Oh, and before you go . . . I want you to take this book with you. It's the Youth's Educator for Home and Society. This will help you understand what's expected of you."

Hedvig took the book and placed it under her arm.

"Do you have anything you would like to ask?"

"No, madam," Hedvig replied as she stifled a yawn. It had been a five-week journey to reach her destination and she was exhausted.

"Then, good night."

Mrs. Langston had requested the top on the Victoria coach down for the tour. A cool breeze off Lake Michigan hinted at the end of summer. Otto looked handsome in his morning coat and top hat. The sound of the horse's steel shoes on the cobblestone streets clattered in syncopated rhythm as the carriage wound its way past the massive buildings.

"There's the home of my dear friend, Mae Hodgkins," she said excitedly as they turned onto Woodlawn.

"She's the only person I will receive unannounced. She has a magnificent ballroom on the third floor of her manor home. It's been the center of many marvelous soirées."

Mrs. Langston continued to drone on about English Tudor and Venetian Gothic and Classic Revival and Frank Lloyd Wright and Stowe. The young servant's senses were overloaded with visions of brick and stone and gargoyles and Italian reliefs. The names of Mrs. Langston's friends all ran together: the Rockefellers and the Harpers, the Goodspeeds and Starkweathers, the Whittons and Robies and Armours. These were men who oversaw industry and the Board of Trade, published books, built universities and railroads. These were the *titans of commerce,* as she called them.

Are there any fishermen or farmers in this neighborhood? Hedvig wondered. What would Mrs. Langston think of the island *she* called home in the middle of the Baltic Sea? What would she think of the tiny stone dwellings and medieval ruins and massive wall surrounding the city of Visby? What would she think of the crumbling, six hundred-year-old limestone cathedrals, an integral part of the landscape?

Hedvig missed her mother and father. Her father's death earlier this year—so sudden! Losing his income from tending the gardens at the church in Klinte on Gotland, as meager as it was, rendered the family destitute. This proud man, so devoted to his family, was laid to rest in a pauper's grave. Three weeks after his death, she was on a ship to America. For her to stay took food from the mouths of her siblings. "You'll have a better life," her mother promised. Oh, how she missed her friends and family. Homesickness overcame her and her heart ached, but she maintained the stoic continence and attentive charm of a true Victorian/Scandinavian woman.

"Were there any visitors while we were gone?" Mrs. Langston asked as she handed the parlor maid her wrap.

"Yes, madam," the servant replied as she reached for the silver salver on the parlor table. The vestibule was so spacious voices echoed and heels clicked on the polished marble floors. Somewhere in the parlor, the sweet song of a canary greeted them.

"I'm expecting Mrs. Hodgkins at ten thirty."

"No need to expect me, Phoebe. I'm here!" her friend called out cheerfully, her hands filled with packages.

"Hedvig, please take the parcels from Mrs. Hodgkins."

"Yes, madam."

"My coachman is bringing the rest. Where do you want these placed, dear?"

Mrs. Langston thought for a moment and said, "Let's take them to the parlor. These will be wonderful hostess gifts for this afternoon's tea. Let's place them on the table nearest the window."

"I don't hear the canary singing anymore, do you?" Mrs. Langston asked with fear in her voice. She looked at the open cage door and ran to the brocade curtains, shaking them wildly.

"Scat! Shoo! You bad cat!" Fur bounded across the couch and down the stairs. "Oh, that poor little bird!" she sobbed.

Hedvig started toward the rattled woman when feathers flew directly into her hair. Hedvig let out a scream and, with arms flapping, ran wildly through the room. The bird chirped and she yelped until she felt a strong man's arm grab her around the waist and gently pluck the tiny bird from her hair.

All three women stood in a state of shock. Finally, Mrs. Hodgkins regained enough composure to say, "Miss Svenson, I'd like you to meet Mr. Arton, my coachman. Mr. Arton, this is Miss Svenson."

John gave a slight bow and with a wide grin replied, "Miss Svenson, you're the only woman I've met with naturally fly-away hair."

One Month Later

Mrs. Langston affectionately squeezed her friend's gloved hand. "It's been too long since I saw you last."

The impeccably dressed woman rubbed the small of her back, "Four hours in a carriage, and I don't care how new the coach . . . is torture on dirt roads."

"You'll have to tell me all the news from Lincoln Park once you've had a chance to freshen up," Mrs. Langston replied and handed the visitor's satchel to her newest staff member.

"Miss Svenson, please escort Mrs. Von Huff to the guest room at the top of the stairs.

"Yes, madam," the young ladies maid replied.

Sunlight streamed through the gauze sheers in the guest room. Crisp white linens and a light gray spread covered the bed. The leaves on the maple tree outside the window filled the pane with hues of red and yellow and burnt orange. A sure sign winter's bitter cold was soon approaching. Another week and the summer linens and drapes would be replaced with the heavier velvets and woolens hung to keep the bitter cold of the barren months of winter at bay.

A small secretary table with personalized stationery and pen sat opposite the dressing table. Hedvig poured water from the pitcher into the bowl and placed a monogrammed towel next to it. A tortoiseshell brush and comb set lay next to the hand mirror.

"Is there anything else you need, madam?"

The stately visitor casually looked around the room. Her hand caressed the yellow spider mums in the silver vase on top of the dresser. "That will be all."

"Yes, madam," Hedvig answered and took the back stairs to the kitchen.

The parlor maid held the salver within Mrs. Langston's grasp. A calling card of refined paper and raised lettering lay prominently in the center of the dish. "Your niece Abigail is—"

"Is what?" the twenty-something woman said as she appeared on the heels of the maid. "Hello, Auntie!"

Phoebe looked surprised, "I thought you were in Europe!"

Abigail draped her hat and wrap on the servant's arms without acknowledging her presence and placed a glancing kiss on each of her aunt's cheeks. "I got bored."

She admired her looks in the mirror on the far wall and pivoted to show off the Italian leather cinched corset encrusted with semiprecious stones.

"Do you like it?" she asked. "I saw it at the fashion show in Milan last month."

Hedvig returned from the kitchen with the silver tea service and freshly baked scones. Without thinking, she'd popped one of the tiny morsels in her mouth before climbing the kitchen stairs. She paused to swallow before Mrs. Langston or the guests saw her. It was her first pastry for the family, and she wanted it to be perfect, to taste as good as what her mother used to make.

"Do you have a new maid?" Abigail asked with an air of distrust. "I think I see her lurking near the staircase. They're all domestic spies, you know," Abigail said in the direction of the narrow servant's hallway. "I've never met one I could trust!" she hissed.

"Hedvig is a sweet, young woman with impeccable credentials. I would appreciate you not showing your ill-breeding in my home with that kind of talk," Mrs. Langston said in a hushed tone.

"And on whose side of the family is this trait of ill-breeding prominent, Auntie . . . my mother or your brother?" Abigail ran her fingers across the piano keys. "Remember when I graced your guests with an impromptu recital?" she said with a grin.

Mrs. Langston nodded, trying to hide a frown, and changed the subject.

"Speaking of brothers, did Randall and Justin come back with you?" she asked, hoping the answer was no.

"Randall and Justin are in New York. I'm sure they send their love."

"Your father is gravely ill, Abigail. The three of you should be with him, helping him."

"Please, I am begging you, please, don't nag me. He's been gravely ill for years."

Phoebe looked at her with disappointment in her eyes.

Abigail dropped her head. "Oh, all right, you win. I'll stop on my way to the cottage."

Hedvig's hands began to tremble from the weight of the tea service. She walked into the parlor as Abigail said, "You know, Auntie, you've got to be more cautious. These crude little peasants have grand ideas of becoming *some*bodies in America!"

"And they *will* be *somebody*, Abigail," Mrs. Von Huff said as she returned from the dressing room. The countess was all too sensitive to the plight of the émigré, being one herself.

"So nice to see you, again, dear. It's a shame you have to leave so soon. It feels as though you just arrived."

Hedvig, her face flushed with shame, placed the service on the table and turned to walk Abigail to the door. A tear glistened on her cheek. The countess placed her hand on Hedvig's arm to stop her.

"Please, Mrs. Langston, it will be my pleasure to see Abigail to the door."

"I wouldn't think of denying you," Phoebe responded.

"Hedvig, please, stay here," Mrs. Langston asked as her guests departed.

She looked the young girl in the eyes and said with a sigh, "I want you to know, no one else in this family is as rude and disagreeable as my niece and her two brothers. I do not share those ugly opinions. Please accept my apologies for her poor behavior."

"Yes, madam," Hedvig replied, the stinging barbs still wounding her heart.

CHAPTER 13

1896

Dare to Dream

"I hear you met Abigail," Otto said with a chuckle as he and Hedvig sat in the horse arena at Mrs. Hodgkins's estate. Hedvig just rolled her eyes. She saw John Arton enter the ring and offer Emma Langston his hand to mount her Tennessee Walker. Sophie Hodgkins, her best friend and schoolmate, was already up.

"John has a reputation for being one of the best coachmen and horse trainers in Illinois," Otto said. "Did you know he rode with Buffalo Bill Cody before he came here?"

Hedvig looked surprised. "Is he a cowboy?" she asked.

Otto laughed out loud. "Actually, his family's quite wealthy. His grandparents on his mother's side are the lord and lady of Bjärsjölagård Castle in Skåne.

Hedvig looked faint.

"They're not royalty," Otto hastened to add. "Nils Johnsson earned his status as a horse breeder and trainer for the king's cavalry. John spent a lot of time between his family's farm and the castle when he was a boy. But he had a dream to come to America, and he gave up everything to follow that dream."

"Keep your head up, Miss Langston! Where you look is where you'll fall," John shouted after the novice equestrian. His hands clapped out the cadence for horse and rider.

"Miss Hodgkin, sit-a-bump! You're on the wrong shoulder."

He watched her for a moment then replied, "That's much better."

"There's talk of a large party next month," Otto said after a long pause. "Is that true?"

Hedvig didn't know if she should respond or not and squirmed uncomfortably.

"The news is all over Hyde Park," he said casually.

Hedvig took a deep breath and blurted out, "Fannie Merritt Farmer from the Boston Cooking School will be guest chef at Mrs. Langston's dinner party. She's published a new cookbook with standards for measurements! I just can't imagine using anything other than these," she said as she held her hands up in defense of the old ways.

Otto had a smug look of satisfaction on his face because his new friend said more than she should have. Hedvig felt used.

"You tricked me!" she said, realizing he could make her life miserable if it got back to Mrs. Langston that she had shared the big surprise. She could hear her mother's warning: "Don't be so impulsive! The Bible reminds us, 'the tongue lives in a very slippery place.' Watch what you say and to whom you say it."

"I will never tell you anything again!" she vowed as she tried to hide the fear she felt.

"The secret's safe with me," he said and crossed his heart.

"Class is over," Emma announced as she rode past. "Sophie and I are going to cool the horses down in the outside paddock."

John was sitting on a three-legged stool in the tack room when Hedvig and Otto walked in.

"Miss Svenson," he said as he continued polishing a bridle with hog's lard and beeswax salve.

"Mr. Arton," she responded in kind.

"Where are my manners?" he muttered as he offered her his seat.

"I see you finally finished it," Otto acknowledged with a nod toward the stool in John's hand. "John's been studying furniture design," Otto explained. "He's a furniture maker *and* inventor and a mighty fine one at that."

Hedvig's hand followed the curves of the stool.

"This is just a practice piece," John stated sheepishly. His tan cheeks flushed from the attention.

"This barn stool was made with the same precision as a refined piece of furniture," Otto continued. "Someday, you'll see . . . Mr. Arton will be famous for his furniture designs."

"Very nice," Hedvig replied.

Before John could respond, Otto asked, "Did you see today's paper? Ferris died! He was only thirty-seven years old."

"Is this a friend of yours?" Hedvig asked.

"No," John replied. "George Washington Gale Ferris was a brilliant mechanical engineer."

Otto handed her the morning's newspaper and pointed to a picture of the Ferris wheel.

"What does it do?" she asked.

"It does nothing," John answered. "It's a ride."

"The most incredible ride ever assembled," Otto added with pride. "Over a million people rode it during the Columbian Exposition back in 1893."

"Did you ride it?" Hedvig asked the two men.

"We'd stand in line all day for one go around. It didn't matter that it cost fifty cents a turn," Otto replied with a laugh as he pulled his pockets inside out. "We'd go home broke!"

"It took nine stops to fill the thirty-six compartments," John explained. "Once they were all filled, the conductor allowed the wheel to make one full rotation. It took twenty minutes to go all the way around. These compartments were so large that each one held sixty people at a time."

"While at the top, you could see all of Chicagoland," Otto added with a wide sweep of his hand. "If you turned to the west, you'd see Buffalo Bill Cody's Wild West Show on the Plaisance just outside the White City."

He crouched near Hedvig and gazed into the distance. "Right in front of your eyes, there'd be stage coach robberies and Indians and wagon trains and cavalry! You could barely breathe for all the dust and gun smoke!"

He put his arm around John's shoulders, "My friend introduced me to Buffalo Bill Cody and Annie Oakley, the best sharpshooter that ever lived!" he bragged as he counted off the celebrities on his fingers. "I even said *howdy* to Chief Iron Tail, who was part of the Congress of Rough Riders of the World. He was a real live Indian straight from the plains. He wore two eagle feathers in the braid trailing down his back, buckskins, and all!"

The giggles were coming closer to the tack room door. "The horses are in the standing stalls, Mr. Arton," Sophie said.

"Thank you, Miss," John replied as he filled two wooden buckets with oats and a mixture of carrots, beets, and turnips. "Your next lesson is Wednesday!" he called after the girls.

Mrs. Langston, clutching a letter to her bosom, waited for her daughter's carriage to arrive at the porte cochere door.

"Emma, we need to leave for South Carolina tonight. I'm sorry to tell you this, but your Uncle Sam passed away." She handed the girl the letter to read for herself.

Emma ran her finger across the black stripe framing on the envelope before she opened it. Everyone dreaded receiving correspondence in these formally stenciled wrappers because the message inside spelled doom. Her hands trembled and tears fell freely.

"Ingrid is packing our luggage as we speak," Mrs. Langston said as she held her sobbing daughter. "Hedvig, pack your things and meet us in the kitchen. Karna is making us box lunches for the ride. Otto, we depart for the train station in half an hour."

Phoebe and Emma Langston sat quietly on the over-stuffed leather couch in the lawyer's office. Hedvig placed glasses of water on the table nearest them and quietly moved to the far corner of the room. Abigail stared out the window at the carriages traveling down the cobblestone road three stories below. Her monogrammed hanky, crumpled in her hand, was dry to the touch, even though she sobbed with every mention of her father's name. Abigail's two brothers paced impatiently.

Vultures, Phoebe thought. *They are all vultures. Sam, you deserved better than this.*

Mr. Yates, his arms filled with estate files, opened the door with a nudge of his knee. "Please sit. We have a lot to go over, and most of it you won't like," he said with a stare over his glasses at Sam's three grown children.

Mrs. Langston motioned for Hedvig to sit.

The attorney tapped the end of his pencil on the desk until everyone was seated before he began. "In essence, Sam's financial assets will be equally shared."

The kids exchanged glances barely containing their glee. They knew their father's estate guaranteed them a lifestyle of privilege and ease until their last breath.

Yates cleared his throat and continued.

> ". . . with the following dictate. I bequeath my full fortune to my only niece, Miss Emma Langston, to be paid to her in equal parts by my two sons and one daughter."

Yates explained, "In other words, I will hand you these checks and quit claim documents and you will sign them over to your cousin through her guardian and legal counsel," he said as he pointed to Mrs. Langston and himself.

Sam's offspring stared at each other in shock.

"But . . . but that means . . ." Justin stammered in disbelief, "we have nothing!"

"In regards to the family business, I imagine my father wants me to—" Randall began to say.

"As a matter of fact," Mr. Yates interrupted,

> ". . . a portion of the company shares will be distributed to the employees."

He looked over his glasses to the paper in his hand.

> "Mrs. Phoebe Langston will hold 51 percent ownership of the shipyards and all other business

holdings until such time as Miss Emma Langston reaches the age of consent."

He sighed and took a sip of water. "If there is any objection by any one of the children, that means you, and you, and you," the attorney said as he nodded toward each of the stunned heirs, "if you object," he began to read:

". . . you will be obligated to donate one thousand dollars to the Sisters of Charity for each complaint."

Mr. Yates looked long and hard at each child as he handed them copies of their father's last will and testament. "Are there any objections?"

Hedvig lowered her head out of respect for the deceased and wished to be anywhere but here. *How sad,* she thought as she discreetly looked around the room at society's elite. She thought of her own family and all they suffered after her father's passing. Even though her family had little in the way of earthly possessions, they stood solidly in their love for each other, willing to sacrifice for the sake of family. Hedvig had grown to love and respect Mrs. Langston and her daughter. If nothing else, this experience taught her money can't buy love.

Sam's children stood in isolation, their backs to their aunt and cousin. The young servant lowered her eyes and thought, *Being poor may be a blessing after all.*

The long silence ended abruptly when Abigail stamped her foot and sobbed, "Ooooooooh, Daddy!" Her beautifully monogrammed hanky now stained with real tears.

BEGOTTEN: With Love

CHAPTER 14

1902

Sparks Fly

"Get away from that window," Karna scolded.

"We're just enjoying the beautiful view," Otto replied with an impish grin.

Kirsten giggled and whispered to Otto, "He just kissed her."

Karna ran to the window and pushed the two gawkers away. "Can't you give them a little privacy?"

She pulled the corner of the curtain back and spotted the lovebirds standing under the rose garden's arched gate. The light from the dining room silhouetted their figures in the shadows.

A quartet from Bredfield's orchestra was entertaining Mrs. Langston's dinner guests with strains from Sidney Harris's waltz, "Meet Me at Twilight." The perfect ending to the wonderful meal prepared by her host chef.

"Uh-oh," John said as he held Hedvig in an embrace.

"I think our friends saw that." Conscious of placing her impeccable reputation in jeopardy, he said, "Slap me."

"Ow," Karna gasped from the kitchen window and grabbed her cheek. "That must have hurt!" She dropped the curtain and hurried toward the range.

"Act natural," she said frantically. "They're coming!"

Otto picked up a spoon. Kirsten grabbed it from him.

"Here . . . try this," she said as the couple walked in.

"Yum," he replied while his whole face contorted. "I've never tasted anything quite like it!"

Hedvig looked at the pot and then at Otto. "I'm not surprised. That's Mrs. Langston's herbal face mask. She lets it steep on the back of the range until bedtime."

"Needs more honey," he said with a shudder and a laugh. He quickly looked for a towel and the pitcher of Roman Punch Ingrid made earlier.

He poured a small glass of the watery ice and lemon juice, which included a mixture of sugar, egg whites, and a jigger of rum. It had a reputation as a palate refresher between courses. Hopefully, it would help him now.

The ninth bell on the panel of bells in the hall next to the kitchen shimmied the summons for the guests' coachmen. "The Hodgkins are taking their leave," John said to the group as he rose from the servant's table and grabbed his top hat.

"Otto, did you reserve the carriage from Drexel Stables for tomorrow?"

"It'll be waiting for you," he assured his friend. "Hedvig and I can't wait until you pick us up," Otto said as he batted his lashes.

Hedvig blushed and busied herself cleaning the sink full of pots.

Clear skies and gentle breezes . . . ideal picnic weather, John thought. Hedvig's hand trailed beside the dingy as he slowly rowed across the lagoon.

"Look over there," he said, pointing to the far shore. A Canadian goose and twelve goslings swam in and out of the cattails clustered near Wooded Island. The bird's mate stood guard on the slope next to the water's edge.

Hedvig bent the rim of her hat to shield her eyes from the sun. "Aren't they adorable!" she said as the balls of yellow down bobbed close to their mother.

"They mate for life, you know," John said and immediately wondered why, of all things, he said that!

Hedvig gave him a sideward glance and looked beyond the bow of the tiny wooden boat.

"Look at those magnificent stairs leading into the water."

"That's Field's Columbian Museum. During the expo, it was the Palace of Fine Arts. Visitors arrived by gondola at the base of those stairs. Masterpieces from the finest art museums all over the world, including the Vatican, were a part of the collection for that year."

The boat slid silently through the water and slowly drifted toward the base of a massive stone bridge: to the right were the walking trails of Wooded Island; the left, the palatial museum; beyond, the deeper waters of Lake Michigan.

John knelt in the boat. His arms flung wildly like a choir director at the crescendo of the "William Tell Overture." "There's where the machinery and electrical buildings stood. Unfortunately, they were destroyed in a fire. The mechanical arts building was south of here. The women's building housed handcrafts from nations around the world, even the US Navy brought items back from South America and Africa."

"Imagine this whole area," he said with the voice of a visionary and a gesture that swept the full horizon, "every building plastered in white and lit . . . with electric lights. A push of a button . . . and you had light! No more smell of gas. No more fear of fires from candles or oil lamps. One day, in our near future, Chicago will be as bright as midday, but it will be midnight!"

"It sounds magical," Hedvig responded.

"It's more than magical! Every man from every walk of life had a chance to step into the future, to see and experience the inventions of today as they apply to tomorrow. The Columbian Exposition was the world's nursery where ideas were born and presented to the public for the first time! Those who attended witnessed the most ingenious sparks of creativity throughout our world, right here, in the White City in every language and culture imaginable."

John took Hedvig's hands into his own. "This is why I came to America. I want to be a part of that. To invent things that will make our lives better. Most people think inventors are a little crazy because most of our experiments fail, but I read where Thomas Edison said: 'I haven't failed, I've just found ten thousand ways that won't work.' And look at what he invented by trying one more time. It just shows you . . . we must keep trying. America is a land of extraordinary people. Anyone—rich, famous, poor, young, or old—can build on their dreams and ideas. And if they don't quit or give up, their discovery can make a difference for the rest of us. Sure, some people will become wealthy because of their contributions and some may lose a fortune. The money earned is a nice bonus, but it's the satisfaction of knowing you made a contribution to society, and maybe even your country, that really counts."

Hedvig peeked at John from behind her parasol. Her hat, the one she bought from Barbour Millinery on Forty-second Street, was carefully placed on her lap. The blue grosgrain ribbon and cluster of springtime flowers matched the ribbon around her waist and the muted floral pattern of the Edwardian lingerie dress she wore. She looked at John and her heart skipped a beat. He was so handsome . . . and wise . . . and passionate. When they were together, she could barely speak! What was the matter with her? She couldn't wait to see him; she thought of him with her every waking breath. She even dreamt of him and what it would be like to be his wife. But he barely noticed her . . . in that way.

John stretched out and basked in the beauty that surrounded him. His long, lean body belied the nerves beneath. What was the matter with him? He was trained in martial arts, tamed horses, rode in Buffalo Bill Cody's Wild West show, and crossed an ocean in the cargo hold of a ship! Why did this woman turn him into a prattling schoolgirl?

Two firm pulls on the oars and the boat slid smoothly onto the narrow slip of sandy shore next to the bridge.

"The air is filled with the scent of roses," Hedvig said as she breathed in deeply. Her arm nestled the crook of John's arm and they strolled through the garden on Wooded Island.

"This reminds me of my mother," she whispered as she held a bloom between her fingers. "Mama was happiest when she tended her flowers."

Hedvig and John's wedding portrait

John fumbled in his pocket, searching for the box with the white gold, filigree-cut ring. The delicate setting held two side diamonds and a center pearl. He'd carried it with him for three years, waiting for just the right moment.

He gulped as he gazed at Hedvig sitting on the park bench overlooking the lagoon and the granite-paved beach beyond. Her beauty was as delicate and perfect as the blossoms.

John's hands began to sweat and his mouth went dry. He began to stammer when the tap from behind startled him.

"We're going to set up for the picnic," Otto said as he held the hand of his wife. "Are you coming?"

John looked at the ring . . . looked at Otto . . . looked at Hedvig . . . looked at the ring . . . and wondered, *Would there ever be a perfect time?*

CHAPTER 15

1904

The Parcel

John carefully opened the small parcel from Sweden, grateful it found its way to his new address. He'd meant to notify the post office but . . . oh, well. No harm.

"Hedvig!" he shouted. "Come see what the family sent!"

His words echoed through the partially filled rooms of the second-floor apartment in a three-flat on Osgood Street in Chicago. The near north side neighborhood kept the newlyweds close to John's job in furniture manufacturing and surrounded them in an enclave of immigrants from Scandinavia. The cluster of ethnicity eased the transition from the old country to their new homeland through the Independent Order of Vikings (IOV), a group dedicated to helping aliens adjust to a new culture. John and Hedvig, servitude contracts fulfilled, enjoyed their emersion into the American lifestyle.

Boxes from their recent move, neatly stacked along the dining room wall, spilled into the foyer. His bride set the armful of pans she unpacked on the kitchen table and joined him on the settee in their sunroom.

Hedvig's natural beauty, impeccable manners, and quiet charm filled every room. She never cursed. She never expressed anger nor busted a gut laughing either. Stoic summed it up: *unmoved by joy or grief and submissive to natural law,* as described in *Webster's Dictionary.* She found contentment in the moment. A Svenska Flicka by birth, an American by choice. She was an ambassador for the realization of the American dream for European women of her generation.

"Meet your in-laws," John said. "These were taken the week before I came to America."

Arton Clan with friends – Ahlestatorp, Sweden

She studied the pictures for a long time. The Arton siblings resting in the side yard next to the manor house at Ahlestatorp made her realize how vastly different their backgrounds were.

Her family lived modestly in a tiny, stone cottage on the grounds of the Lutheran church in Klinte. The largest city she'd ever visited as a child was the walled city of Visby, forty miles away. She and her siblings were mesmerized by the ruins of the medieval cathedral known as Saint Catherine, a favorite place for them to play while her family sold fish and produce at the fresh market next door. The narrow, cobblestone streets surrounding the ruins led to the north entrance of the imposing buttress and the ancient fishing harbor beyond.

Hedvig's childhood home – Gotland, Sweden

The wall of the city was built around 1,500 AD, not to protect the elite from invaders, but to keep the poor within from mingling with the wealthier class outside the walls.

John studied the face of his wife and hugged her tightly. "My family may have achieved a certain amount of wealth and prestige, but we are still farmers. You know as well as I do that in Sweden you don't have an opportunity to move beyond your station in life."

Arton kids prior to John sailing to Amerika

John pointed to his brothers and sister one at a time. "This is Sven, a wonderful artist, photographer, and inventor. Next to him is my brother, Anders, a master landscape architect who has designed major parks throughout Skåne. Sitting below him is Nils, the comedian of the family. One day he'll write a book and become famous . . . it's just a matter of time. Next to him is the baby of the family, my little sister, Caroline. We call her Leena. She's studying dermatology and dreams of coming to America. Then, you recognize that incredibly handsome man. Oh, that's me! And sitting is my youngest brother Pehr, a machinist. My sister, Hannah, took the picture. She's the sensible one in the family, the rock. The one we all turn to when common sense is needed."

Hedvig handed the family picture back to her husband.

"John, did you read the note on the back?"

"No," he said, as he took it from Hedvig. He mumbled in Swedish as he read Sven's well-formed cursive script and leapt to his feet.

"Sven and Leena are coming to America!"

"When?" Hedvig asked.

He muttered as he read more. "And Pehr, it says here," his finger trailing the words as he translated from his mother tongue to English.

"When?" she asked, again.

He looked at her, not sure of the response when he said, "And maybe Nils."

"When?" she firmly repeated.

He looked at the postmark and then at her.

"This was sent three months ago!"

"John, when are they coming?" Hedvig asked again as the doorbell rang.

He sheepishly smiled at his wife and walked to the door.

"They may be here."

CHAPTER 16

1920

Patience Pays

Hedvig sprawled across the couch in the front parlor. It was a beautiful, wine-colored settee her husband brought home as a Christmas present from Marshall Field's department store last year. She caressed the velvet material with her hand, following the pronounced curve of the back. It was an exquisite, Victorian piece designed by one of John's friends. A smile crossed her face as she thanked God for her family and all the blessings in their lives.

It was early afternoon, and Hedvig's face glistened with sweat from carpet sweeping the oriental rugs in the living and dining rooms. The smaller rugs hung on the line in the backyard. Her arms and back ached from the workout.

"Oy. Oy. Oy," she whispered under her breath as she caught sight of herself in the hall mirror.

Her auburn hair fell across her shoulders, raining down past her waist. Less than a year ago, her hair swept the tops of her ankles. John did not want her to cut it, but she couldn't stand the headaches from the weight any longer. Slow but sure, she was cutting it . . . a little at a time.

It was April in the Windy City. Melting slush lay piled in patches in the shadows and canyons of the tall steel and stone buildings.

"Good afternoon, Mr. Mulcrone," John greeted the trolley driver. He was surprised to see his regular driver at this time of day.

"How's the family?" Ed asked as he eased into traffic with a clang of the bell.

"We are all well," John replied. "And yours?"

"Why thank you for asking, Mr. Arton. Kate's a little tired these days with three kids and a new baby," he grinned and handed John a cigar. "That's why I'm working extra shifts—I need the rest!"

"Congratulations," John said as he took a seat behind the trolleyman. The men talked about family and politics and sports for the twenty-minute ride.

"Your stop's coming up, John," Ed said as he slowed the trolley and John leapt from the car. He was in a hurry to get home.

Andersonville, a predominantly Swedish neighborhood on the far north side of Chicago, bustled with immigrants from Foster on the South to Bryn Mawr on the north, Broadway on the east to Ashland on the west. It was the neighborhood of prestige for immigrants enjoying financial success.

"God middag!" Mr. Hansson called out cheerfully as John approached the floral shop.

"Good afternoon to you, as well," John said in perfect English, hoping to encourage Mr. Hansson to speak in his new tongue.

"I'd like a bouquet for my wife," John said as he entered the shop.

Even though he was breathless from the long, city-block walk to his front door, John decided to take the steps three at a time to the family's third-floor apartment.

"Hedvig!" he shouted, waving a large manila envelope in one hand while holding the bouquet of spring flowers in the other. The buds took a beating as he grabbed the stair railing to pull himself along. A puff of petals laid in his wake as the tender shoots slapped the wall with each pull.

"Hedvig!" he shouted again. It was early afternoon, not the usual time he came home. He couldn't wait until evening to tell the family his news.

"Hedvig, where are you?" he shouted again as he searched from room to room.

"I'm in here, John," she said, scurrying to throw on a clean housedress and comb her hair before he found her. Her hand fumbled across the dressing table, searching for hairpins.

"You're home early," she called out as she applied the only hairpin she could find.

"Here, these are for you," John said as he handed her the bouquet of broken stems and battered leaves. One lone daisy teetered on the end of a split stem. She took the gift and laughed as the daisy and her hair both fell to the ground.

"What is in this envelope will change our lives forever!" John said to his wife and two young daughters, Verna and Vera, as they sat around the kitchen table.

"Papa, please don't tease us any longer!" said Verna, a pixie-ish, preteen with sparkling blue eyes and chestnut brown hair.

"This is the new Bed Chair design patent!" He announced and shook the packet. "I've been waiting four years for this patent application to be approved."

Even as they applauded, confusion clouded the faces of the young girls.

"Do you know what this means?" he asked.

"No, Papa," said seven-year-old Vera as she twisted a blond ringlet of hair.

"This means . . . ice cream for everyone! Go get your coats."

"Yay, Papa!" The girls squealed and ran to the front hall closet.

He watched his children and at that moment grasped the joy his father may have felt, if he were still alive, knowing John could now provide a comfortable home and future for his family, just as Anders had done for John and his siblings all those years ago.

"This design will revolutionize hide-a-bed construction, Hedvig," he said as he showed her the mechanical drawings. "Anderson Manufacturing is giving me exhibition space at the Furniture Mart for the National Furniture Manufacturer's Association Show in July. They're expecting thousands to attend over three weeks."

Patience Pays

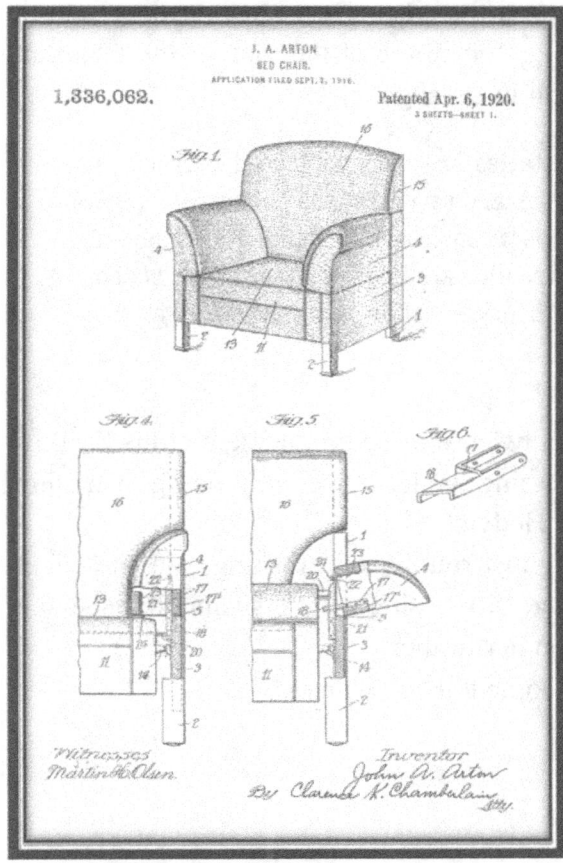

Bed Chair design patent

He held the drawing toward the light. "Hedvig, this is the big break we've worked toward all these years!"

Hedvig hugged her husband. "I am so proud of you," she said as she reached for the day's mail.

"This came for you. I thought it might be important," she said as she passed the magazine to her husband. John scanned the cover of the May 1920 issue of *The Furniture Worker's Magazine*, but he was too excited to read it.

"I talked to Mr. Frewburg today about that shipment of steel I've been waiting for. He said the railroad strike should end any day now."

"Come on, Papa," the girls begged as they pulled on John's arm. He reached for his suit jacket and bowler hat.

"We know Mama wants vanilla," he said as he put his arms around his girls, "and what would you like?"

His jacket sleeve grazed the magazine pages, opening it to the centerfold. The following story forecast the tone of the upcoming months for manufacturing in Chicago:

> 'The davenport factories are inconvenienced very much by the railroad strike, and several of the plants are on the verge of ceasing operations. Cars containing a supply of steel interior construction are tied up in freight yards and cannot be moved. Every effort is being made to get the cars through.'

That night as John crawled into bed, he looked at his beautiful wife sitting at her dressing table. "Are you doing something different with your hair, Hedvig?"

She stopped her nightly routine of brushing and pulled her tresses over her shoulder. "I'm using a new shampoo," she said, hoping he didn't question her further.

"It looks nice. Now come to bed, woman."

CHAPTER 17

1923

Hidden Treasure

"Look at that line of people, John!" Hedvig said as they turned the corner from Clark Street into Lincoln Park.

Elm and oak trees dotted the grounds near the gently curving sidewalks of the nation's oldest zoo located on Chicago's near north side. An elaborate series of lagoons meandered between exhibits.

"Do you see that?" Hedvig asked the children. "Look, above the tree tops . . . that's downtown," she said, pointing at the skyscrapers south of the park. "That's where Papa works."

A lion bellowed on the other side of a boulder jutting from the landscape. Startled, Vera grabbed her big sister's hand as they approached the cat house cautiously. Hedvig kept close to her girls and warned them not to stick their hands over the fence, even though a deep moat separated them from harm.

Ten-year-old Vera pointed at the mane on the beast sprawled under a bare wood tree and said with a chuckle, "That lion's hair looks like yours when you wake up, Papa!" Her sides shook with laughter.

"Very funny," John said as he self-consciously smoothed his thinning locks.

"This path goes to the new aquarium," fifteen-year-old Verna said as she followed the signs and crowd to the exhibit.

"I'm sure the story of five run-away sea lions walking into a restaurant on Clark Street is pure lore, but . . ." John paused. "What about the one that got away?" he asked playfully.

"It's over there!" Verna squealed as she poked her mother in the ribs.

Hedvig jumped.

"What *is* that over there?" John said more to himself than anyone else.

Hedvig motioned for the girls to follow as John led the way.

In a corner of the lagoon, under an A-frame tarp was a boat, neglected and full of bird droppings. Overgrown with climbing vines, it looked abandoned. It was barely noticeable to passersby.

"If I didn't know better, I'd say this is a Scandinavian longship."

"Our teacher said it came from Norway," Verna replied.

"Norway!" John scrambled around the wooden vessel, looking for any identifying marks. He brushed the rambling vegetation on the steel bar fencing to the side.

A small sign read:

"THE RAVEN"

VIKING LANDFINDER

REPRODUCTION OF A 9TH CENTURY VIKING SHIP

"I know this ship," John said. His voice cracked with excitement. "Its true name is *Viking*."

"Why does the sign say *Raven*?" Vera asked.

"When this ship first landed in America, a bright red pennant with the outline of a black raven flew from the bow. The press mistakenly called it Raven and the name stuck. They didn't know that a raven is an important symbol in Scandinavian lore."

"What does *lore* mean, Papa," Vera asked.

"It's a story that teaches an important lesson," he explained, realizing his girls were still only children and knowledge is wasted if not understood.

John sat on the lawn next to the ship. "Girls, this is a replica of the ancient longship Gokstad. Captain Magnus Andersson convinced the king of Norway to let him build and sail a replica of the Gokstad to America with a crew of eleven. It was presented as a gift to the good people of Chicago during the Columbian Exposition in 1893."

"You see, it's been argued for centuries that it wasn't possible to travel that far in something so small," said Hedvig.

"Scandinavian history was passed on orally, so there were no documents to prove that Leif Eriksson . . ." John began to say.

"Do you mean Erik the Red, Papa?" Verna asked.

"No," John replied. "It was his son, Eric the Lucky, who landed in the new world six hundred years *before* Columbus."

"Did this ship prove it?" Vera asked.

"We can now say the stories passed down from one generation to another are not myth."

Vera looked at the small vessel and with hands on hips asked, "How did they get here? Where are the paddles?"

"Aaaah!" John said. "When this Viking ship sailed to the steps of the Palace of Fine Arts in Jackson Park Lagoon, a large-striped, woolen sailcloth was secured to the mast in the midsection. The hull displayed thirteen shields on each side with eleven oar ports set between. See?" he said as he pointed to the holes on the second strake (plank) of the fragile wood.

"There was a beautifully carved dragon head set on the prow and a fluted tail at the stern," he said with sadness as he looked at the stubs of oak worn smooth from years of neglect and harsh weather.

"It took the twelve men forty-four days to travel from Bergen, Norway, to Chicago under sail and manpower." His back hunched as he pulled on the imaginary oars. "Thousands lined Lake Shore Drive as the Gokstad came to port. It was an amazing sight!"

John reverently caressed the side of the ship. "I had a chance to ask one of the sailors how fast this little ship was under sail. He told me it could do more than ten knots."

"What ever happened to the sailors?" Hedvig asked. "Did they stay in America or return to their homeland?"

"I don't know," John said and asked the girls, "What do you think?"

"I think they stayed," Verna responded.

"I think they missed their homes," said Vera.

Hedvig and John exchanged glances. "You're right. They would miss their homes and their families. Maybe some of them stayed and some of them went back to Norway."

"It's a big decision to give up everything and come to a foreign land," John said.

"Our teacher says not everybody is welcome in America. Is that true?"

"She's right!" he nodded.

"Why?"

"Because not everybody who comes here wants what's best for America."

John pulled a blade of grass and set it between his front teeth. "Hedvig, do you remember when President McKinley was assassinated? The man who shot him was an anarchist," John said, shaking his head. "That man had not grasped the beauty of this country's politics. He didn't believe in the balance of justice and power."

"Our government has a responsibility to protect us from our enemies," Hedvig said.

"Congress made laws stating who will and won't be admitted and what will happen to them if they mean us harm," John added.

"Why did they place quotas on immigrants two years ago?" Hedvig asked.

"America is meant to be a blend of nationalities and religions. Remember, we're a melting pot of ideas and talent from all over the world."

"Just like a good stew depends on the right amount of spices and herbs," Hedvig replied, "our country needs the right balance of ideals."

Verna looked at her family and held her belly. "Talking about food makes me hungry, Mama. Is anybody else hungry?"

"Can we go to the Red Roof Café?" Vera asked as they joined the crowd on the main path.

"Sure," John said, "but I just want to say one more thing . . ."

The girls looked at their father and rolled their eyes.

"Consider this food for thought," he said as he playfully tousled their hair. "We're a country that believes in liberty and laws based on God's teachings. You won't find that anywhere else in the world," John said with conviction. "Our constitution and way of life are worth defending. Never forget it."

BEGOTTEN: With Love

CHAPTER 18

1926

Vikings' Valhalla

Wave after wave of Swedish immigrant families carefully picked their steps from the train platform on top of the hill, down the grassy slope, and onto the lawn of the forty-two-acre estate in Gurnee, four miles west of Waukegan and fifty miles north of Chicago.

John and Hedvig stood on the veranda of the two-story Georgian manor house overlooking the grounds. Hedvig gaped as she gazed at the massive crowd spilling from the train cars.

An eighty-by-eighty-foot square dance platform in the side yard was filled with partiers bobbing their heads in beat with the Waukegan Glee Club's a cappella harmonies, truly a pulsing sea of humanity.

"Roger Turner from *Lakeland Press*," the young man said as he extended his hand to John. "Do you mind if I ask you a couple of questions for an article on the dedication?"

John looked at him intently but said nothing.

Undeterred, the reporter asked, "What brought you here today?"

"This is going to be our home someday," Hedvig exclaimed.

"Have you toured the interior?" the writer asked, pen poised.

Hedvig's cheeks flushed with excitement. "The rooms are filled with sunlight. Each window overlooks the beautiful grounds. I think it will be a nice home with all the amenities we would ever need!"

John whispered in her ear, "Who wound you up?"

"What?" she said as she cupped her ear and smiled.

"How many people are here today?" John asked the young writer.

"Ten thousand, according to the police chief . . . maybe more."

"John!" yelled a familiar voice. Otto ran to greet his old friend.

"Thank you for your time," the reporter said to Hedvig and walked away.

She smiled and turned to greet Otto's wife.

"Wait until you see who's here," Anna said, smiling back.

Hedvig caught a glimpse of their friends from the Ladies Independent Order of Svithoid FRIA Four and the Ingebord Ladies of Drake Lodge.

"We'll be back," the ladies said to their husbands as they made their way into the swarm of women.

John turned to his friend and said, "I was hoping you'd make it."

"Look what I have," Otto said, pulling a handful of change from his front pocket. The shiny new Buffalo nickels spilled from his palm into John's.

"Look who's on it," he said as he pointed to the profile of Chief Iron Tail.

"Well, I'll be," John said in dismay. "Doesn't that bring back memories?"

Otto stared at the image on the silver coins carefully. "We have rubbed elbows with history, John. Ain't that something? Who would've thought when we were fresh from the old country, and you were riding with Buffalo Bill Cody, that Chief Iron Tail would someday be etched on an American coin?"

"Imagine that," John replied and began to hand the nickels back to Otto, but his friend motioned for him to keep them.

Out of the crowd, a tall, stocky man with a shock of blond hair and high cheekbones stopped and stared at John.

"Excuse me," he said politely, "but didn't you design the convertible sofa?"

"Yes," John replied.

"I saw your picture in the *Tribune* last Sunday. We have one of your hide-a-beds in our living room and love it!"

"Thank you for telling me that!" John replied. "There's a matching chair, you know."

"That turns into a bed?"

"It does," he said. "Come to the studio next week and I'll show you." John offered the stranger a business card. The man thanked him, turned to his wife, and the two faded into the mass.

"Looks like life's treating you well," Otto said.

"And you . . ." John responded. "I don't call all my friends doctor."

Otto smiled modestly.

"I have a little gift for us," John said mysteriously.

His friend waited patiently as John slowly pulled an envelope from his pocket. "Mr. Anderson gave these to me yesterday."

Otto folded his arms over his chest and waited. Finally his patience ran out. "What is it?"

"These!" John said with a big grin as he held up two tickets to the first ever Army/Navy football game to be played at Soldier's Field in the fall.

Otto threw his hands skyward and shouted, "If I hadn't married my wife first, I would have married you!"

Hedvig and Anna shook their heads and gently pulled the men toward the dining room. Posters lined the walls. A large board told the history of the Independent Order of Vikings. Pictures and renderings highlighted the activities of the lodges, and brochures scattered on the tabletops boasted of the building of the Vikings' Valhalla.

IOV Drake Lodge – circa 1900

"Did you ever see a finer group of Vikings?" Otto asked, pointing at a poster of immigrants dressed in attire from their native land: metal helmets, medieval weapons, and traditional clothes.

"No, and we probably won't until that final longship transports us and our Valkyries to the true Valhalla."

"It makes sense that we take care of our own," Anna said.

"I don't ever want to be a burden to anyone, especially my children," Hedvig replied.

"The whole purpose of the IOV is to provide a sense of community for the Swedish people and to help those less fortunate by offering insurance and death benefits," said Grand Chief Johnson from Brage Number Two Lodge, who had overheard their conversation. He handed the men a packet of information.

"This will explain the increase in assessment fees, due to the maintenance of the Vikings' Valhalla home for the aged."

"How much of an increase?" Otto asked.

"When you get your next notice, you'll be asked to pay one dollar a year for the upkeep on this home."

"That's double what we pay now!" Anna exclaimed.

"And forty years from now when you're a resident, it will be just as beautiful then as it is today."

I wouldn't mind living here when I'm old and frail," Anna replied.

"We'll be neighbors then," John said. "I've already picked out my room."

"You can't sleep in the kitchen, John!" Hedvig teased.

"Close enough," John said as he opened the door to a model room right across the hall.

BEGOTTEN: With Love

CHAPTER 19

1929

Sugar Bowl Economics

It was a brisk walk from the apartment to the church: a chance to greet friends along the way and catch up on neighborhood news. John and Hedvig enjoyed the weekly ritual, especially during the summer before the weather turned muggy and hot. Chicago could be brutal in August.

"Paper! Get your paper!" the young lad shouted from the street corner newsstand. "Thank you, sir!" he said as he handed John the morning edition.

"Look," John whispered to Hedvig. There it was . . . a picture of Mr. Hansson sitting in his 1927 Cadillac Convertible being pulled by a horse! The headline: "Hoover Wagon Grassed to Go!"

"I can't believe what's happened to the Hansson family. His beautiful store, closed!" Hedvig said as they passed his shop.

A lone ceramic pot lay on its side in the window, partially hidden from view by a lace curtain. The long butcher-block table stood in the middle of the room, meticulously cleaned. Vases stacked in rows on the shelves, according to size and color, sparkled in the morning sunlight. A wicker basket tucked on the shelf below the workbench held a rainbow of colored ribbon.

"This was his dream," she said, running her fingers along the gold-stenciled lettering on the window of the door to the flower shop. "I thought he was doing so well!"

"He was," John said, folding his arms across his chest.

"What happened?"

"The bank wouldn't lend him the money he needed to upgrade the plumbing in the building. The city insisted it be done or they'd put a lien on his property. If there's a lien, the bank considers him high-risk, even though his credit rating is good." John paused and shook his head. "They wouldn't even talk to him. Instead of helping him, the bank foreclosed. Now, he and Hannah are unemployed *and* homeless."

Hedvig noticed the shades on the Hansson apartment windows above the store were pulled down, a good indication either the flat was empty or they weren't receiving visitors. She sighed.

"Hannah told me they're using the horse to save gas. If they lose the building, their hope is to drive to Minnesota and live with her brother. He owns a farm outside Minneapolis."

"The bank froze their assets until Hansson pays the mortgage in full. If he can't, everything will be sold at auction, including the car," John said sadly. "That's why the neighborhood's holding a rent party for the family this evening."

"Nobody, in this day and age, in this great country, should go hungry or lose the home they've worked so hard to purchase," Hedvig said bitterly.

A stifling August breeze drifted through the back door screen of John and Hedvig's apartment. Twilight turned to darkness, and lightning bugs filled the sky with spasms of pulsating light. Hedvig finished packing the apple pies she baked for the party while John sipped his coffee and scanned the business section from this morning's *Chicago Tribune*.

"From what I've been reading, the crisis is beginning to ease," he said. "Stock prices fell last March, but they've picked up all summer."

Hedvig stared at him in disbelief.

In his defense, John added, "The larger lenders like Goldman Sachs and City Bank are investing again, with vigor."

"Say what you will, but I disagree!" Hedvig said as she ladled the oxtail soup into bowls and placed a piece of homemade, buttered Rye bread on their plates. "People can barely afford necessities, much less luxury items. The butcher told me most of his customers rely on credit to get by. They're falling behind, but they're either too far in debt, too proud, or too foolish to start living within their means. Nearly everyone we know is one paycheck away from disaster."

"We're fortunate," John said. "I've worked for Anderson Manufacturing for years. My designs boosted company sales, and the owners offered me shares in the company in payment for my inventions. I was even mentioned in the *Furniture Worker's Magazine* in June for my seventh patent."

"Then why have employee wages and hours been cut in half in the last three months?" Hedvig asked.

"It's just a temporary measure to help stabilize the company's assets, I'm sure. We'll weather whatever comes our way," John said reassuringly.

"Thank goodness we don't owe anybody anything." Hedvig replied. "We pay cash for our debts. We have savings in the bank.

And when we're old, we'll have a roof over our heads at the Vikings' Valhalla home."

"Uh-huh," John mumbled. He was a cautious man . . . most of the time; he never kept a secret from Hedvig, until now. He knew she wouldn't understand his purchase of two thousand shares of Anderson Manufacturing stock last summer, not with the wild fluctuations in the market. The concept of stock margins and dividends, commodities and splits, portfolios and divestitures and derivatives were beyond her understanding, in his estimation. He wasn't so sure he understood them himself, but he wasn't about to admit it.

Her concept of money wrested on basic Sugar Bowl Economics: You save it, you spend it. You use it . . . you replace it.

Someday, he'd tell her about his investment when the market was more secure. Someday . . . when the gamble paid off. Not today.

"If President Hoover doesn't do something to get this economy moving soon, we may all be standing in a soup line," she said.

With his nose back in the paper, John replied, "You're right, dear."

Hedvig poured a second helping of soup in his bowl and asked, "John, did you hear a word I said?"

"Of course I did," he said with genuine surprise. "I agreed with you. The soup's delicious."

Swedish / Scotch / Irish / English
Blended History

CHAPTER 20

1942

Love and War

Battleship gray skies camouflaged the position of the USS Wolverine thirty-five miles out from Chicago on Lake Michigan. The ground crew drew their pea jackets close, a welcome barrier from the bone-chilling squalls. The squadron of F4F Wildcats from Glenview Naval Air Station just north of the city was somewhere in the soup: maximum air speed 320 mph; cruising altitude 19,800 feet. Ten-foot swells rocked and pitched the paddlewheel aircraft carrier, a 1913 converted steamer outfitted to train the navy's flyboys.

Tom heard the distant drone of 1,200 hp Pratt and Whitney super-charged, single engines from the flight deck. Pratt. A familiar name to Tom. He heard his grandfather mention Daniel Pratt often. But this was not the same Pratt who founded the Cotton Gin Mill town of Prattville in Alabama. This was another industrious man living the American dream. No relation to the Pratt that hired Tom's grandfather straight off the boat from Scotland. This was another Pratt, as ingenious as the bold entrepreneurial, Daniel Pratt, who inspired Adam Weir to open the Western Slope Foundry in Grand Junction, Colorado.

The first wave of planes appeared out of the low-hanging mist flying in tactical formation. Filled with patriotic pride, a prayer of resolve passed Tom's lips as he vowed to keep our men in the air. General quarters sounded. *This is a drill. All hands on deck!* Swabbies snapped to as *Touch-and-Go* training maneuvers began.

Later that day and back on land, young servicemen swept through the streets of the city, weekend liberty passes in hand.

Anna Verna Olivia Arton

Verna shouldered her way through the crowd at Mayor Kelly's Servicemen's Center on Wabash in downtown Chicago. Even though the calendar said May, the unusually cool temperatures begged a wrap for warmth.

"Hi, Ginger," Verna said to the hat check girl as she sidled up to the cloak room counter.

"Did you make that?" the girl shouted over the music as she looked at the powder blue cable knit cardigan with popcorn stitch buttons.

"I finished it last night," Verna replied as she quickly modeled it before handing it to the girl.

"Oh, that's swell!" Ginger said and draped it on a hanger. "Say—somebody told me you're offering knitting classes. Is that true?"

"Next Sunday. Lorraine's got all the particulars, if you'd like to come." Verna's voice trailed off. "Wait a minute!" she said as her hands quickly searched her purse. "Did I leave anything in my sweater's pocket?"

"Sure 'nuff, honey," Ginger said with a big smile and handed her the black armband with the USO insignia.

"Thanks, dear."

Lorraine sat in a corner of the canteen, a sewing kit and spools of thread on the table. The line of service men grew as word spread that she could sew the newly earned hash marks on a uniform. She held court in the same spot every week and had come to know many of these young recruits by name.

"Hi," Verna said as she breezed past the line of sailors.

"Here," she said to Lorraine as the packages she had balanced precariously on her arm slid from her hands onto the table. "The icebox cookies are from Mom.

Tom Weir/Elliott

"Oh, sorry," Verna said sheepishly as she stumbled over the sailor's foot seated across from Lorraine and landed on his lap. "Oh, sorry!" she said again and flushed. The line of men whooped and whistled as Tom helped her up.

"Verna Arton, I'd introduce you to Tom Elliott, but I see you've already met," Lorraine said with a laugh. "Tom's stationed at Navy Pier."

"Are you one of our pilots?" Verna asked.

"I keep 'em in the air," he said.

"What does that mean?" Lorraine asked.

"I signed on as an aviation chief metalsmith."

The girls looked at each other with confusion written all over their faces.

"Well," he said as he offered the ladies a cigarette, "I worked at Roah Aviation in San Diego before I enlisted. The navy thought I knew how to keep the wings on their birds, but once they found out I was doing it with bobby pins and chewing gum, they decided to send me to school to learn how to do it right."

"He just got here from San Diego a week ago and doesn't know anyone," Lorraine explained.

"Well, now you know us!" they said in unison and laughed.

"You'll have to excuse us," Verna said. "We've known each other since junior high."

"So, you're city gals?"

"Born and raised," Lorraine said.

"San Diego's not so small," Verna added.

"I was born and raised in Colorado," Tom answered.

He pointed to the middie in his hand. "I'm going to put this in my locker. When I get back, I'd like it if you'd dance with me," he said with his gaze fixed on Verna.

She blushed and replied, "I'd like that."

"He's such a nice guy," Lorraine said after Tom left, "but such a sad story—not even thirty and a widower. Can you believe that?"

"What happened?" Verna asked.

"His wife died from childbirth complications."

"That's awful! Did the baby survive?"

"Yeah, her parents adopted him. With the war and all, there's no way Tom could raise a baby by himself."

Verna saw him coming towards them and smiled. He was lean with dark, wavy hair and light, blue-gray eyes. His voice was deep, and his accent hinted at a southern/western drawl. He had a rakish grin.

He tipped his hat to his brow and held out his hand. She took it and followed. On the dance floor were 1,200 servicemen and 800 junior hostesses jitterbugging to Glenn Miller's "Chattanooga Choo-Choo." Tom and Verna made their way into the mix.

"Hedda Hopper's column in the *Chicago Daily Herald* today said this is the first song to sell one million copies," Verna said, trying to shout above the music.

"What?" Tom said as they completed an under-arm turn. Verna just smiled and shrugged. The smell of his aftershave . . . intoxicating.

His arm on her back and the gentle pressure of his hand around hers signaled his intentions: rock-step, triple-step, cuddle-up; rock-step, triple-step, rump-roll, slide. Their steps were quick, small, and in sync.

"Where did you learn to jitterbug?" Verna asked.

Tom bent toward her ear and said, "My little sister. And you?"

She looked at him with surprise, "*My* little sister!" she answered with a giggle.

Tom breathed in deep. Her perfume . . . intoxicating.

BEGOTTEN: With Love

CHAPTER 21

1942

Romance and Roller Coasters

Hedvig and Verna stripped the last of the ripened green beans from the victory garden in Vera's backyard. "I heard on the radio this morning that 40 percent of America's produce is being grown in home gardens like this one," Hedvig said.

"We're lucky to have a small patch where we can do our part. Aren't we, Mom?" Verna said as she fanned herself with her hand. It was humid this morning, a foreboding of a typical Chicago summer day.

"Does Tom like salad?"

"He's not a fussy eater," Verna replied, plucking a large, red tomato off the vine.

"Will you be here for dinner?" Hedvig asked as she pulled a handful of scallions and carrots and placed them in the basket.

"I think so. Vera and I are going to meet Tom at Riverview. A few hours in this heat should be enough."

Nine-year-old Myrna and six-year-old Lloyd stood on the back porch, pounding on the railing. "Come on, Aunt Verna, we're going to be late!" they pleaded.

"Did I mention we're taking the kids?" she said and smiled.

Myrna and Lloyd ran to Tom, who was waiting near the ticket stand, while Verna and Vera strolled to the entrance of the expansive amusement park.

"Did you ask her?" the kids whispered excitedly as they nervously looked over their shoulders toward their aunt.

"Not yet," he said. "It's a secret, so shhhhhhh!"

The kids pulled their mother towards the gaping hole of Aladin's mouth at the Castle's Fun House. Puffs of wind lifted the skirt of an unsuspecting patron as a small crowd of servicemen and teens stared and cheered. Myrna and Lloyd crowded around the fun mirrors and laughed as their legs shortened and bellies extended in their contorted reflections. A push forward with their faces and their chins drooped to the ground.

"Do you want to come with us?" Vera asked.

Verna shook her head. "Tom wants to go to the Bobs first. He wants to see a *real* roller coaster."

"Okay. We'll meet you at the Pair-O-Chutes in an hour," Vera replied.

"Come on, Mom!" the kids shouted as they ran for the line.

"My friends and I used to come here all the time when we were in high school," Verna told Tom. He walked in circles, taking it all in. He had never seen a midway as beautiful as this. The park took up seventy-four acres of prime real estate in the heart of Chicago's residential area at Belmont and Western, less than a half-mile from Lane Tech High School on Addison Avenue.

"The Bobs is a wooden roller coaster with an eighty-five-foot vertical drop!" Verna said, her eyes as round as the ride tokens in her hand. "It sits on the Chicago River. One turn is so violent, you think you're going to end up in the water!" she said as her hand made a motion straight down.

"Are you trying to scare me?" he asked as he put his arm around her shoulders.

"I bet you scream like my little niece!" she said, pointing straight ahead of them. "There it is. . . ."

Romance and Roller Coasters

The creak of wood and ratcheting groan of gears warned of predicted shrieks as the cars inched their way to the top of the ominous, white structure.

"We'll see who hollers," he said, puffing out his chest.

"Step right up," hawked the strongman standing outside the entrance to the Bobs. His skin-tight leotard with red and yellow lightning bolt stripes on a field of blue magnified his muscles.

"Win a Kewpie doll for your sweetheart!"

The giant grabbed the sledgehammer, and with all his might hit the disk at the bottom of the pole that contained the weight. It shot straight to the top. The clang of the bell from the collision of metal on metal pierced the air on the midway like the sound of a bullet.

"How about you, sailor?" he shouted out to Tom. "Did ja eat your spinach today?"

"You want a Kewpie doll?" Tom asked Verna. She nodded her head with enthusiasm.

"You heard the lady," Tom said as he picked up the sledgehammer. "Phew, this is heavier than it looks!"

Tom tried to steady the hammer over his head, tottering to the right and then the left. The forming crowd gave him a wide berth as he swaggered in their direction. He put the hammer down and walked around the pole.

"I don't know, honey. I think I need a kiss for luck!" he said as he stuck his cheek towards Verna's lips. She closed her eyes and puckered. He quickly turned and stole the kiss and walked away flexing his muscles.

"Any pointers?" he asked the strongman.

"Yeah . . . let her do it!"

The crowd laughed as Verna shook her head no and took a step back.

Tom defiantly stared at the carnival barker, picked up the sledgehammer with one hand, and swung. He hit the platform squarely. The weight hit the bell with a loud, resounding clang.

"That was quite a show!" Verna said as she took her prize and hugged Tom.

"Thanks, Pete," Tom said to the strongman.

"It's good to see you, Tom."

"How do you know—" Verna began to ask.

"Pete was my roommate when I worked the carnival for a season in California. We were both nineteen."

Pete looked at Verna and asked, "Is this the missus?"

Tom held her hand and said as he got on bended knee, "Verna is the love of my life, and I would be most honored if she would be my wife."

Verna's face registered surprise. "You have to ask my father's permission!" she demanded.

"He already did," John replied as he stepped out of the crowd.

"Dad!" she shouted, and then she saw her mom, sister, and the kids. "You were all in on this?"

"We've all said yes," Hedvig laughed, "but I think he wants to know what your answer is."

"You may want to talk to me first," Pete interrupted. "I roomed with him for a summer, remember?"

Verna threw her arms around Tom's neck and yelled, "Yes!"

The kids scooted around the lovebirds as the family walked the midway.

"Dibs!" Myrna shouted as she spotted her favorite steed on the seventy-horse carousel, a prancing palomino with an ornate saddle and brightly colored ribbons streaming from the bridle. Vera hoisted Lloyd onto a charging black Arabian. The front hooves pawed in midair; its open mouth strained at the bit. Tom and Verna sat on a bench nearby, sharing a box of Cracker Jacks, oblivious to the cacophony of screams coming from the stomach-churning rides in the park, rides with names like: The Comet, Flying Turns, Fireball, and Chute-the-Chutes.

"You realize when we get married, it means you're going to be a navy wife."

"I know," the thirty five year old said. "I've been pretty independent most of my life. I'm not looking forward to us being separated, but I'll do you proud."

"I'm not a rich man, and right now things are a bit tight," Tom shared. "I send money home every payday to help my mom and brother."

"What's wrong?" she asked.

"Times are tough," Tom said. "I told you after Mom and Dad divorced, she eventually remarried. He was a wonderful man but died suddenly, leaving her with a baby to raise by herself."

"That would be your sister, Babe, right?"

"Yep." Tom paused to munch a handful of the candied popcorn. "My brother, Spike, joined the navy right out of high school."

"Where's he stationed?"

"He's not," Tom said. Verna was afraid to ask.

Tom and Verna's wedding

"While he was on guard duty, a young recruit went AWOL. He jumped Spike from behind and stabbed him in the neck. He nearly died."

"Oh, Tom, that's terrible," Verna replied, raising her hand to shield the horrified look on her face.

"When he recovered from the coma, they told him he'd never walk again. He's proving them wrong!"

"That's great news!"

"He'll be living with my mom and sister, and I need to do what I can to support them until he regains his strength."

"I understand." Verna said with a reassuring pat to Tom's hand.

Tom, overcome with guilt, hung his head and looked away. He had promised himself he wasn't going to continue this lie anymore. Spike had recovered enough to work at Bay Meadows Racetrack in San Mateo, California, and Tom had never sent a penny to help any of them, not since he was in the CCC. He wanted to . . . God knows he wanted to, but it seemed something always came up, like another beer or two for his friends at the bar . . . any bar.

Verna stroked his arm to reassure him everything would be all right.

He sighed and looked into her eyes. "That's not all," he said quietly. "We're shipping out in three weeks."

Verna could feel the tears well up and buried her face into his shoulder.

"I don't want to wait to get married," he whispered in her ear.

"Neither do I," she replied.

"Oh, Tom, look!" she said as she pulled the toy from the Cracker Jack box. The tin pin, shaped like a sailor, held a large heart with the word ***Taken*** imprinted on it.

"I can't afford an engagement ring right now, honey. I hope this'll do," Tom said with pleading eyes.

"You planned this, too?" Verna asked.

Tom grinned and winked.

"It's beautiful," she responded as she pinned it on her sundress.

Cracker Jack token

CHAPTER 22

1947

Sea Stories

Three black Fords rumbled down the gravel street, throwing dust and stones in their wake. Even at three years old, the little girl knew when her father drove down the road, it was sixteen hundred hours.

"Daddy's home!" Joanie shrieked as she ran to the edge of the driveway. She waited patiently until the cars rolled to a stop. Tom pulled closest to the home's cedar-shake wall and slowly opened the door.

"Daddy!" the little girl squealed as she ran to her father with open arms.

Tom hoisted her onto his shoulders and walked toward the house; his buddies followed. The tiny child could see the whole world from up there! She thought her daddy was the strongest, most handsome man in the whole wide world.

"Verna, we're here!" Tom shouted as he opened the front door a crack. "We'll be in the back."

Verna brought a tray of snacks to the yard. "Hello, boys," she said with a wink.

Tom and buddies

Tom placed a washbasin filled with ice and beer on the ground in the shade of the apple tree next to the Adirondack chairs.

Wes settled back and reached for his pack of cigarettes rolled in his T-shirt sleeve.

"Hey, Gunny, you got any *!#*#! matches?"

"Not in front of the kid!" Tom hissed as he motioned toward the house.

"Sorry, Tommy," Wes said, biting his tongue.

He struck a wooden matchstick on the seam of his dungarees, waited for the flame to flare, cupped his free hand around the cigarette, and took a long drag before flicking the spent stick into the bomb casing the boys had converted into an ashtray.

"I don't know . . . but I've been told . . . Eskimo feets are mighty cold!" Joanie began to sing.

The men laughed. They taught her that song last time they sat in the yard drinking beer and swapping tales.

Gunny threw his cap on Joanie's head. White-blond, baby-fine hair curled around the lower rim. Her eyes covered, she lifted her nose high and marched in circles singing another song in her limited repertoire:

"Lep, lep, lep-right, lep . . . I lep my honey and I lep my wife and I thought I was in the right . . . right . . . I write my honey and I write my wife and I write them with my lep . . ."

Hap's little puppy followed Joanie through the yard, tugging on the hem of her jumper.

Verna came to the back door. She didn't say a word, just stared at all of them and shook her finger. Her eyes riveted on Tom and the little girl.

"Go see what your mom wants," Tom said as he pushed the tiny girl towards the kitchen door. The rambunctious cocker followed.

"Come here, Boola," Hap called. The dog looked at its master but chose to follow the child.

"Toss me a beer," Wes said, motioning towards the bucket next to Tom. A fresh cigarette dangled from his mouth. Curls of smoke drifted toward his eyes.

"Scuttlebutt has it Doc's shipping out," Tom said, staring at the ground.

"Where?"

"A flat top in the Pacific."

"I got my orders yesterday," Hap said after he chugged the rest of his beer.

"Where?" Tom asked.

"Kaneohe."

"You lucky SOB!" Wes snorted as he shook his head. "What I'd give to be stationed in Hawaii."

"That's the good news. The bad news is I can't take the dog."

Joanie sat on the porch steps with Boola's head resting on her lap. She gently stroked the puppy's back and laughed when it nuzzled her for more. Its long ears hung to the ground, tickling the little girl's toes.

"Aaaaaaw, look at that," Hap said. The men gazed at the little girl hugging the puppy and in unison stared at Tom.

"What?" he asked as he looked at his buddies and then his daughter.

"Oh, no!" he responded as he shook his head. "Nuh-uh . . . Verna will never stand for it!"

The three swabbies looked at each other and mockingly shook their heads.

"A skirt wouldn't stop me from helping *my* buddy," Gunny said, putting his arm around Hap.

Hap shrugged his shoulders and nodded his head in agreement. "He's right!"

"And look at that sweet little girl," Wes added. "How can you say no to that child?"

Tom held his head in his hands. If he said no, there'd be hell to pay. If he said yes, there'd be hell to pay. Is one side of hell hotter than the other? He'd have to think about it.

The men sat in silence, chugging their beers. Things were heating up in the Pacific Rim again. They knew in the not-too-distant future, they'd all be shipping out.

CHAPTER 23

1948

Atonement

The rain finally stopped. Joanie slowly twirled the pint-sized, glass Mason jar round and round as she sat cross-legged on the front porch. Ribbons of sunlight broke through the green slime and murky water, showing glimmers of tadpoles and egg bubbles floating in the glistening goo.

"Do NOT go to the pond in your new dress, Joanie," her mother warned her sternly. Verna fussed with the ribbons in Joanie's hair, straightened the lace collar, and went back in the house with one final warning, "I mean it!"

The four year old let out a long sigh as she pressed her nose against the jar. When the sun slipped behind a cloud, the murky water darkened even more.

They can't breathe, the little girl reckoned. *They need fresh water!*

She picked up the jar and looked toward the door. Her mother's warning echoed in her ears as she slowly twirled the container one more time. Her mother explained about the angel and the devil sitting on her shoulders prompting her to do good or bad.

I'm not going to stay and play, she reasoned, looking at both shoulders, not sure which one was good and which one was bad.

She sat on the steps for a moment. It wasn't easy to decide what to do. But above all else, she knew she should be careful.

Joanie picked her feet up slowly to keep the mud off her new, black patent-leather shoes. She held the jar away from her body to keep the dirty water away from her party dress.

A sweet, clean smell filled the air. The stones on the road leading to the path were already dry. Meadow grasses and wildflowers arched over the trail that sloped to the water's edge. Joanie held the jar in both hands as she started down the familiar route. As her little legs brushed the plants, droplets fell from the water-laden petals and slickened the already slippery clay path.

One step on the soft surface, and her legs splayed north and south, then east and west. Gravity dropped her to her side and she lurched onto her belly. The jar tumbled end over end until it slapped the surface of the water. It quickly sunk to the muddy bottom. Tadpoles scattered . . . free from the child's grasp.

Joanie slid to the water's edge face down. Dirt and algae clung to her hair and globbed in her mouth. Her dress, the new, white party dress with the itchy lace collar and fluffy petticoat, was now caked with dirt and streaked with grass stains. Her hands bled from grasping the razor-sharp grass along the path. Shaken, she struggled to catch her breath. Her little body shuttered with fear as she tried to imagine the trouble she was in. The need for her mother's hug far outweighed the scolding she imagined.

Joanie limped home, stifling her sobs. Her father was standing on the porch. Her mother stood right behind him. Verna met the little girl on the steps and carefully removed the dress. "Leave your shoes here, Joanie," she said and disappeared.

Tom grabbed his daughter by the shoulder. "Get in here," he growled through gritted teeth. His free arm hung at his side, concealing the suspenders wrapped around his hand.

"I'm sorry, Daddy," the little girl said through her tears, and she meant it.

"What did we tell you?" her father bellowed. His jaw tensed.

His hand rose above his head, and in one single motion, the suspenders wrapped around the child's torso. The metal clasps ripped at the flesh on her arms and legs. The pain tore through her body and sucked the air right out of her lungs. He pulled them off her with a jerk and whipped her again. She felt a curdling screech leave her lips as the suspenders wrapped around her body again. Waves of nausea gripped her and she shook violently.

"Don't ever disobey us again!" he yelled.

The suspenders wrapped and recoiled one more time.

"Tom! Stop!" Verna screamed.

Joanie felt her body crumble and her world faded to black.

BEGOTTEN: With Love

CHAPTER 24

1948

Keeping Peace

Verna stood in the bedroom doorway, hoping her daughter was asleep. She loosely knotted the tie on her floor-length bathrobe and nervously looked toward the kitchen.

Joanie loved that robe, with its splashes of brightly colored, tropical flowers on a field of white. She learned to identify colors while sitting on her mother's lap. It had been a gift from Tom when Verna and Joanie met him in Hawaii for his previous tour of duty. It had been a year since they were all under the same roof, and that roof was attached to a duplex on Ford Island in the middle of Pearl Harbor. Even though the war ended five years earlier, remnants were still visible in the harbor, including the Arizona, which had become a shrine for so many of our military men.

Now, the family was back on the mainland, and all that was left were memories.

"Verna!" Tom called out, his voice thick and speech slow.

"Shhhhh. I'll be right there," Verna called back in a voice barely above a whisper. A shudder ran through her, and she pulled her arms around her waist in an attempt to compose herself.

"I know you're awake, Joanie," Verna said as she approached the bed.

Joanie could not figure out how her mother could tell. The little girl squeezed her eyes shut as tight as she could. In the distance, the faint sound of *pop . . . fizz* made it clear her father had opened another bottle of beer.

"Get that kid to sleep and come here!" he slurred.

Verna's hands shook as she pulled the covers around Joanie.

"Do not get up, sweetheart, no matter what," she instructed. "Do not cry out, no matter what."

She kissed Joanie on the cheek and left the room. The sweet scent of her perfume lingered. The fragrance usually calmed the young girl, but not tonight.

Joanie heard a slap and a sob and her mother plead, "Oh, Tom, no!"

Even with her pillow over her head, she could hear furniture scrape on the bare floor, the rip of material, and the sickening thud of flesh hitting flesh, again and again.

If I hold my breath, Joanie thought, *maybe it will stop.* But it didn't. She wished she could remember the prayer her mother taught her. But she couldn't.

"Amen!" she'd say with a quivering voice. "Amen, Amen, Amen!"

Her sheet wet with tears. Her sobs muffled by the pillow. The house went silent and soon she fell asleep, exhausted from fear.

Morning light filled the bedroom. Tom was gone. Joanie could see her mother sitting on the couch, reading the paper. She ran from her bed to her mother's lap and hugged her as only a four year old can. She squeezed her mother so closely she couldn't see her wince.

"You get dressed," Verna said as she placed the child on the floor, "and I'll get your breakfast." The battered woman slowly walked to the kitchen.

Joanie never walked anywhere. It was more a hop and a skip. A silly little dance step befitting a Swedish/Scottish/Irish lass. The English blood in her veins kept her feet on the ground around adults, sometimes.

The built-in closet extended across the west wall of the bedroom. It rested on a two-drawer base, which, when the drawers were opened (one a little more than the other), allowed Joanie to climb up and reach her clothes by herself. After all, she would start kindergarten in the fall. In order to keep her balance, she'd hang on her mom's dresses as she reached for her own.

We must be rich, the little girl thought as she wobbled to and fro, clinging to the belt on her mom's nicest dress. *I have three outfits I can wear.*

Mrs. Dixon, the neighbor across the street, told Joanie she was so poor, she'd stand in front of her closet every morning, looking at the one dress she owned, and ask her husband, "What shall I wear today—the new one, the blue one, or the one I wore yesterday?"

Joanie liked Mrs. Dixon. She served her tea, and they'd sit on her front porch in those large wicker rockers and talk and rock and talk. She decided to visit her after breakfast this morning . . . after she got dressed. Mrs. Dixon let chickens run in her yard!

Sometimes, Joanie lost her balance reaching for her clothes. This was one of those days. She fell into the closet headfirst, still clenching her mom's belt.

"Joanie!" her mother yelled from the other room.

"I'm okay," the little girl shouted back, trying to right her body from the tumble. She'd landed in the far corner of the closet on top of Verna's bathrobe. The crumpled gown was thrown in the corner like a used napkin from an all-night diner.

Joanie picked up the sleeve and quickly realized as she held it to her cheek that it was no longer attached to the rest of the robe. It still felt soft and smelled like her mother, but each beautiful patch of color was merely a shred of what it had once been. She picked up another torn piece and held it, breathing in deeply. She picked up another and another until her arms were filled with the tattered robe.

This was the beautiful wrap Verna wore when she read Joanie a story or held her when she had that recurring nightmare of falling through the steel grids of Deception Pass Bridge into the churning water below. This housecoat with the large, colorful flowers . . . the same one she wore through the yard on her way to the outhouse to empty the honey bucket.

Joanie buried her head in the fragments of cloth as tears freely welled and spilled. She felt her mother's arms pull her close and slowly begin to rock her as Verna quietly whispered, "It's okay. We're okay."

Verna with the honey bucket

"Joanie," Verna whispered as she gently shook the child awake. "Daddy's leaving."

Joanie nestled in his arms and took in the heady smell of Old Spice. His freshly shaved whiskers rubbed rough on her cheek when he kissed her.

Verna carried the sleepy girl to the living room window and turned out the lamp so they could see outside. Tom was merely a shadow in the mist in his CPO dress whites, his duffel bag slung over his shoulder. The bright, red glow of a cigarette danced near his lips as he took a long drag. He walked to the end of their property, then past Dixon's homestead, and up the hill to Forsythe's general store. There were no streetlights, just a hint of purple dawn on the horizon.

The bus came . . .
the bus left . . .
and he was gone.

Tom and Joanie Elliott

BEGOTTEN: With Love

CHAPTER 25

1948

Family Matters

The sun was streaming in the living room window next to the couch, a welcome and rare sight for island life in the Puget Sound area of Washington State. Fog usually blankets the ground until noon. Verna mindlessly wiped the same spot on the counter top as she stared out the window above the sink overlooking Thirty-sixth Street.

"Mommy, there's somebody at the door," Joanie squealed.

The four year old jumped from the kitchen chair, still munching cereal, a dribble of milk in the corner of her mouth. Verna wiped her hands on her apron as she grabbed for the tyke.

"Joanie, get down from there," she hissed at the tot scrambling onto the couch to peek out the front door window.

"Mommy, no!" the child whined as her mother licked her fingers to smooth the bangs out of Joanie's eyes before opening the door. Her baby-fine hair swirled to the side of her forehead, plastered by her mother's spit.

House on 36th Street; Anacortes, WA

John placed the two brown suitcases on the stoop next to Hedvig and stood back to look at the dilapidated house and overgrown yard.

Hedvig clasped her hands in front of her and waited for someone to greet them. She watched the handle jiggle with no success before Verna opened the door and reached for the dignified old woman. The embrace tipped Hedvig's pill box hat and bent the feather adorning it.

"Oh my!" Hedvig cried, and the two women laughed. Tears and hugs flowed freely. Joanie hid behind the couch, not knowing who these strangers were that made her mother cry . . . and laugh!

Verna took Hedvig's hand and motioned to her father to follow.

"Come in! How was your bus ride?" she asked as she led the two into the kitchen of the small, three-room house.

The strangers piled their coats on the couch, burying Joanie in the heap. She snuggled into the black one with the soft, lamb's wool collar. It was still warm and smelled much like her mother.

Verna shoveled a scoop of coal into the converted, wood-burning range and filled the percolator with fresh coffee and water.

"I'm so glad you're here! I didn't know where else to turn," Verna said, tears filling her eyes.

"You did the right thing," John replied.

"We can talk about this at length . . . later," Hedvig added as she glanced towards Joanie.

"You're right. I just wanted to say: thank God for family!"

Verna pulled Joanie close and forced a smile to hide her tears. "Remember the letters we write to Grandma and Grandpa every week?"

Joanie looked puzzled.

"You sign them with an X and O."

The little girl nodded, "And seal them with a kiss!"

"Yes you do."

"A big smooch," the little girl said as she blew a kiss to everyone in the room.

"Well, you won't have to write any more letters. This is Grandma and Grandpa."

"It is?" The little girl responded cautiously as she stared at the old couple.

"They've come to live with us," Verna explained.

"They have?" Joanie said as she slowly walked around the three adults sipping their coffee. She began to dance around the table with a big grin on her face. Suddenly she stopped and ran to the front door.

"Where are you going?" Verna called after her and quickly followed.

The child stood on the stoop, looking skyward.

"Where's Santa?" she asked excitedly. "Is he coming to live with us? Where will the reindeer live?" she asked as she wrung her hands.

"What are you talking about?"

"I wrote him a letter, too. Remember?"

BEGOTTEN: With Love

CHAPTER 26

1949

God Jul

"The Christmas tree is here . . . the Christmas tree!" the little girl shouted as she jumped up and down and clapped her hands in excitement.

"Move to the side, Joanie," Verna said firmly as she pointed to that universal spot all moms point to when they try to get their children out of the way. "Grandpa needs plenty of room."

Joanie stood next to the door, straining her neck to see the full length of the nine-foot tree. Verna held the door open, and with one final tug, Grandpa, the tree, *and* the sparrow that had nested on the front porch since the beginning of spring flew into the house.

Frightened by the commotion, the bird darted from wall to wall, leaving dust spots the size of baseballs: one, two . . . above the couch next to the door; three, four . . . over the chairs under the window. Eighty-year-old John jumped after the speeding bird like Rabbit Warstler stretching for a high fly ball in the infield. Hedvig yelped as she covered her head with her apron and ran towards the kitchen, flapping her *Hi Alice* arms to keep the bird away from her hairnet.

Verna pushed furniture out of John's way as the bird landed on the piano's keys in the far corner of the room. Slowly, he inched his way toward the tiny bird, but before he could pounce, it took flight.

"Eeeeww!" Verna cried out as she wiped up the splat of poop it left behind.

The frightened sparrow clung to the ceiling light chain, beak opened wide, chest heaving, gasping for air.

John calmly whispered, "Hedvig, get me a dish towel."

An arm appeared in the doorway. With a flick of her wrist, she tossed the towel in John's direction.

Startled by the motion, the bird flew through the air towards the door and collided with the towel. A collective gasp quickly turned to screams as the bird escaped and continued its frantic getaway. One final poof of feathers near the ceiling, and John captured it. The family huddled together and watched as the sparrow lingered a moment in John's open hands before disappearing into the winter sky.

John slowly dragged the Christmas tree to the corner of the living room and wedged it between the piano and davenport. Its branches bent to accommodate the massive tree's presence in the small room. One bough covered the back of the sofa like the arm of a suitor waiting for his lady. The treetop curved toward a faint smudge spot near the ceiling where the sparrow's wild flight was nothing more than a memory written in dust on the pale yellow wall.

John wrestled the trunk into a battered bucket. Two rough-cut pieces of two by four wedged it in for stability.

"Now, Hedvig?" he asked as Verna and Hedvig scrutinized its straightness. "A little to the . . ." Hedvig began to say for the tenth time.

John's arms began to shake, and he answered with a booming, "Woman!"

Verna and Hedvig looked at each other, knowing it was *straight enough*, even if it were horizontal to the ground.

"It looks straight, Dad," Verna responded.

Hedvig gave a nod of approval. "It looks straight right where it is, John."

"Are the branches going to get fatter?" Joanie inquired.

"What do you mean?" her mother asked.

"The branches—they're skinny, like me. Becky's tree is fat with shiny beads and beautiful lights that bubble. Will ours look like that?"

Verna looked at her for a moment and then responded, "No. This will be a very special tree. One you've never seen before and probably will never see again."

"I don't know, Mom. . . . I don't think Santa likes skinny Christmas trees," Joanie said, hoping the mention of the *big man*'s name would change her mother's mind.

The three women carefully hung the delicate decorations on the spindly short-needled branches (avoiding blisters of pitch) until every branch sparkled.

A smell of cinnamon from the freshly baked Jul cookies blended with the smell of pine from the tree and permeated the home as day turned to evening and a wash of muted sunset colors warmed the walls.

Hedvig's delicate ornaments from Eastern Germany took on a regal prominence between the homemade paper chains and garlands of cranberry and popcorn. Cone-shaped Christmas lights in primary shades of red, green, blue, yellow, and white added a special brilliance to the hand blown orbs. Santa faces and bells, silver birds with spun-glass tails, snowflakes, and candy canes shimmered with Christmas magic.

"This is the most beautifulest tree in the whole wide world," Joanie announced. "Even better than Becky's!"

"Just wait," Verna said with a wry little smile.

John seemed agitated at her remark.

"You'd better make it quick," John warned. He slopped buckets of water on Hedvig's Oriental rug and no one said a word! That rug was her pride and joy. That's what Verna told Joanie after the little girl spilled grape juice on it last week.

"Never, again!" he said, shaking his head.

"Just this once, John," Hedvig assured him as she ushered Joanie out of the living room.

From the kitchen the little girl saw a soft glow settle over the living room. Hedvig crossed her arms under Joanie's chin and placed her hands on her chest to gently hold the child in place. She knew Joanie would bolt if she didn't.

"This is *my* Christmas gift, Joanie. I wanted you to see the type of tree my family had when I was a child," Hedvig said. "Someday, I'll tell you stories about Sweden."

Joanie's eyes widened.

"There were knights and cathedrals, Vikings and longships, Cossacks and cold, cold winter nights . . ."

"Okay, we're ready," Verna called out as she turned on the radio. Strains of Christmas music filled the house.

Joanie held her grandmother's hand as they walked into the living room. All the lights were out. Each branch tip on the skinny Christmas tree held a single, white wax candle. No one noticed John standing on the couch with a bucket of water aimed at the tree.

The soft candlelight flickered stars of light onto the ornaments. A radiance filled the simple, handmade crèche nestled deep within the limbs and illuminated the faces of the Holy Family. The four stared with childlike awe at the creation and their hearts filled with joy and peace. For that moment, all was right in the world.

CHAPTER 27

1951

Across the Miles

"Thanks for the ride home," Joanie shouted from behind her hand-knit scarf as she shut the door to the '49 Ford Jalopy. The eight year old took a quick step back from the hulking fender as Mr. Andrich pulled away. She furiously waved at her friends in the back seat. They waved back, noses and mittens pressed upon the windows.

The afternoon's flurries had grown into a serious storm, unusual for the temperate weather of the Pacific Northwest.

"I'm dreaming of a white Christmas," Joanie sang as she gathered snow in her hands and threw it into the air. She caught the drifting flakes on her tongue as she ran towards the door.

"Hi, Mom, I'm home!" she shouted. A flush of warm air and the smell of baking cookies greeted her.

"Close the door!" Verna shouted from the kitchen. "It's cold out there."

"Cold enough to snow," Joanie said, placing her wet mittens on her mother's cheeks.

"Brrrrrr!" Verna cried and pulled back.

Joanie ran into the alcove next to the kitchen and placed her mittens and coat on the clothes rack next to the wringer washer.

She kicked her boots to the side. A trail of melted snow quickly puddled around them. She loved the mittens her mother knitted from leftover skeins of yarn. Each finger was a different color. No one else had anything like it.

"Wash your hands and you can help," Hedvig said as she slid a tray of raw cookie dough onto the top rack of the oven. She tapped the thermostat on the coal burning range door before deciding whether to stoke the fire or not. The temperature held firm.

Hedvig's bibbed apron grazed the floor and covered the tips of her Enna Jettick shoes. Her dress hiked in the back, exposing the old lady's bowed legs and seamed nylons knotted at the knees. She never wore her girdle when she worked around the stove. Not since she spilled a pan of boiling hot fudge. Trying to free herself from the tight undergarment soaked with burning sugar caused third-degree burns on her belly. That was a lesson she did not want to repeat.

Joanie held up her washed hands for inspection, "I'm ready," she announced. Her mother covered her with a gingham apron and tied the strings into a bow across her chest.

"Sit on the Sears Catalog," Verna instructed. "You'll be able to reach the mixing bowl easier."

"Do I get to squeeze the Good Luck margarine?" Joanie asked.

"Yes," Verna replied as she handed the child the oily brick of white lard.

"Make sure it's all the same color yellow before you stop," Hedvig instructed as she opened the dark dye packet and squeezed the spot of coloring onto the grease.

Joanie giggled at the sucking sounds the glob made when it squished between her fingers.

"Are we sending cookies to Daddy?" she asked.

Verna tapped the side of the cardboard box at the end of the kitchen table and nodded her head.

"T-O-M," Joanie spelled out loud as she traced the letters of her father's name in the air. Blobs of white grease precariously clung to her hands before dropping back into the mixing bowl.

"And what does that spell?" Verna asked as she pointed to the last name on the box.

"Elliott," the young girl proudly answered. "I can write it—do you want to see?"

Before Verna could respond, Joanie dug through her school bag looking for a pencil. A trail of greasy palm prints soiled the pages of her spelling book.

"I made a picture at school today. It's got snow on it. We made it with a toothbrush. Mrs. Smith says mine looks like a blizzard!"

Joanie pulled the crumpled picture out of her bag and smoothed it with her grease-laden hands. "See?" Glitter mixed with the grease as she held the masterpiece up for all to see.

"That's very nice, dear," Verna said and showed it to Hedvig.

"Very nice," commented Hedvig. "Now go wash your hands."

Joanie stopped wiggling long enough for Verna to wipe the last remnants of grease from her hands before she placed them in the warm suds.

"Mom, Mrs. Smith says I'm gonna need a new toothbrush," the little girl said somberly.

Verna's eyebrows jumped to the middle of her forehead, and her eyes narrowed. "Did you take *your* toothbrush to school without asking?"

Joanie's hands slid slowly to her backside, shielding her buttocks as she nodded her head yes but said, "No."

"Would you lie to me?" Verna asked, the tone of her voice edged with doubt.

Joanie's head nodded yes, yet she said, "No."

Verna squatted next to the eight year old and said, "The most valuable gift you have in life is your word. Don't ever lie! Even if you're afraid of getting into trouble, you must *always* tell the truth."

Hedvig pulled the cookie sheet from the oven. The smell of vanilla and warm, buttery dough made Joanie's mouth water. Her eyes pleaded for mercy and a cookie, but Verna held her ground.

"People need to know they can trust you. I must know I can trust you." She took the child's face in her hands and looked her squarely in the eyes and asked, "Can I trust you?"

Joanie put her head down and mumbled, "Yes."

"Did you take your new toothbrush to school?"

"Yes," she whispered.

"Come here," Verna said and took the little girl's hand. She could feel Joanie shake, even though she'd not been physically punished since Tom left.

Calmly, Verna said, "Look under the sink. I have old brushes you could have used."

"I didn't know," Joanie mumbled, feeling ashamed.

"What do we say around here?" Verna prompted, "Use it up . . ."

"Wear it out," Joanie added.

"Make it do or do without," they recited together. Joanie grabbed one of the old brushes, but Verna stopped her from putting it in the holder.

"You can't use that, sweetheart. It has germs. They all do. We'll buy you a new one," Verna said. "But next time you need something, please ask first, okay?"

Joanie nodded.

"I'm ready to start the icebox cookies," Hedvig called from the kitchen. "I can use some help!"

"We need to get that box packed so Grandpa can mail it in the morning," Verna said as she followed Joanie into the kitchen. "We still have popcorn to make!"

John returned from his walk to the post office, shaking snow from his hat and boots. His nose and cheeks were red from the cold. He stood in front of the range and sorted through the pile of cards and letters.

This was the kind of day the kids in town prayed for. The accumulation of snow overnight caused the city to close "R" Avenue to traffic because of the steep incline and slippery conditions. The school buses were not equipped to drive on snow. Classes were cancelled. The hill was theirs!

Joanie watched her classmates climbing to the crest with sleds in tow. Verna handed her the snowsuit hanging from a peg near the back door. She buttoned her sweater, pulled her leggings up, and fought to zip the jacket.

"This is for you, young lady," John said as he handed a rectangular box to Joanie. "And for you," he added as he handed Verna a stack of Christmas cards.

"Can I open it? Can I? Please, Mommy, please?" Joanie whined and danced around her mother while tripping over the snowsuit's shoulder straps she'd forgotten to snap.

Verna cleared her throat and choked out a barely audible, "Yes," before she turned away.

Tears rolled down her face as she handed the card in the red envelope to her mother. She pressed her finger to her lips and rolled her eyes in the direction of the little girl sitting cross-legged on the floor, tugging at the twine on the package.

Hedvig read the colorfully decorated card, stifled a gasp, and walked away, visibly shaken. The brief, handwritten note read:

Merry Christmas!
The baby weighs six pounds, four ounces. Her name is Tomiko.
Tom

CHAPTER 28

1952

Family Lore

Joanie slowly sipped the lukewarm broth, hoping to soothe her throat from the tonsillectomy four days earlier.

"Is Grandpa afraid of doctors?" she asked her mother as Verna poured herself a cup of coffee.

"No," she answered. "Why do you ask?"

"Because when Grandpa had the flu and wouldn't go to the doctor, Grandma said she was going to send him to the vet!"

Verna laughed.

"Do they have hospitals in Sweden?"

"Yes . . . but when Grandpa was a child, hospitals were only in big cities. Ahlestatorp is a farming community," her mother explained. "There were no hospitals close by."

Joanie placed her hand on her still tender throat. "Did he have his tonsils out?"

"No, but when he was a teenager, he needed an operation to save his life."

"What happened?" Joanie asked.

"He had appendicitis," Verna said, holding her right side. "Grandpa was too sick to move. They had to operate at home."

"Did his mom have ether? I don't like ether!" Joanie said, wrinkling her nose.

"I don't think they had ether back then," Verna said, shaking her head. "They didn't have medicines like they do now."

The memory of the doctors and nurses hovering over her with that sieve and piece of cloth over her face—all still so fresh in her mind—a few moments of fear, then a free fall into darkness.

"What did they do?" Joanie asked.

"It just so happened that when your grandfather suffered this attack, the king's cavalry was practicing at the stables a few miles away on the estate where *his* grandfather lived. The mounted soldiers *always* traveled with a medical team, so they came to your grandfather's aid."

"How?" Joanie wanted to know.

"They set up a field hospital outside the family's farmhouse. Grandpa's father made him drink a bottle of whiskey, and when it was time to operate, the doctor gave him a twisted piece of leather to bite on if the pain was too bad."

"Grandpa was very brave!" Joanie replied with a newfound respect for the old man's courage.

"Indeed he was," Verna responded. "The doctors tied him to the kitchen table and they operated."

"Is that true, Mama?" Joanie asked, horrified at the thought.

"Yes, it is."

"How can you tell the difference between a true story and a tall tale like the ones Grandpa tells?" Joanie asked.

"For example, if I told you about Grandpa's operation, and I said this . . ." Verna paused a moment, cleared her throat, and began:

"The doctor tied the young man to the kitchen table and prepared to operate. There was a terrible storm that night: ice and snow and howling winds. Horses and buggies couldn't get through the drifts. Word was, the nurse wasn't coming! They couldn't wait any longer. It was now or never, or the boy would die. But the doctor needed someone to assist with the operation. He couldn't do it alone. So, the young patient volunteered to hand the instruments to the doctor himself!"

"Well, that's just plain silly," Joanie said with an impish grin. "He couldn't help . . . his hands were tied!"

Verna just looked to the heavens and shook her head.

"Mom, what's the difference between a tall tale and a lie?"

"If you tried to convince someone that a tale is actually true, that would be wrong. If you leave it up to a person to separate fact from fiction, and they know from the beginning that it's a story, fine. If they're not sure where truth and fantasy begin or end, then you've woven a good tale. But the point of telling a tale is to teach an important lesson, while entertaining the listener."

"Do all people tell tales?" the youngster asked.

"You'll hear people tell tales all your life! Some will tell stories to entertain you; some will tell tales to influence what you're thinking; and some will tell out-and-out lies to make themselves look good or to hide the truth because they don't want to get caught doing something wrong. It's up to you to learn to tell the difference," Verna said as she handed Hedvig a basket of freshly sprinkled shirts.

"Never be afraid to question what someone is telling you, Joanie," Hedvig said as she continued to iron. "Always search for the truth in everything you do."

"I tell you what," Verna suggested, "let's listen to Grandpa when he starts weaving his tales during dinner tonight and see if we can tell what's true and what's not."

Even at eighty-three, John was a towering man, lean and tan. His snow-white hair and piercing blue eyes commanded attention. He was proud to still have all his own teeth, albeit worn to half their original size and yellowed with age. He never smoked . . . never drank.

John was a master at weaving reality with imagination. Joanie sat mesmerized as John's face captured a scene only his mind could see.

"There we were," he began as he looked at her. "It was hotter than a chili pepper sandwich! Buffalo herds next to the railroad tracks as far as you could see. Traders piled hides as high as the train station's roof. Dust and stench choked the breath from your lungs. Welcome to South Dakota," he said as he crooked his arm and shifted in his chair.

"The Winchester hung limp in my arm. Every cartridge spent . . . yet, the beasts continued to stampede toward the locomotive. They were coming on us, fast! The pounding of their hooves, deafening! There was more ammunition a few cars up. Those of us who could knew we needed to get to the front of that train, pronto."

Grandpa took his time slathering his hardtack with bacon grease. His suspenders rested on his muscular chest; fresh dirt from the garden streaked the thighs of his pants. The earth smelled sweet and rich, mixed with the sweat of hard work. His rolled-up shirt-sleeves exposed the tattered long johns underneath, holes in the elbows, frays on the neck.

John's gaze drifted to the past.

"It was a wet spring that year in Kansas," he said as he started a *new* story.

"Everyone was gathered at the barbershop. It was too wet to work the land and too early to drink. Massive clouds were building. Bird wings flicked a transfigured white in the darkening sky." John's hand began to swish back and forth.

"I listened to the rhythmic slap of the straight-edged razor on the leather strap while I waited for my shave. The world went silent, except for the gasp from the town drunk as he dove through the front door. A raucous sound followed him like the snort of a rodeo bull fast on his heels. Dust and thunder shook the ground!"

John's arms twirled over his head.

"The stick building quaked to its core! Towels and elixirs flew at us and across the floor. Within seconds, it was over. Not one man injured, but the front of the building was totally wrenched from its foundation."

He paused and placed his fists on the table, fork in one hand, knife in the other.

"All there was to see was sky . . . lots of sky."

He placed his hand in front of his face, ducked his head, and collapsed on the floor. Fingertips grabbed the edge of the table as he pulled his eyes level with the table top.

"T-t-t," John spit in staccato, mimicking the drunk. "T-tornado!" he yelled before hitting the floor. Joanie heard a belly laugh as John pulled himself back into his chair.

Joanie never knew from night to night what adventure he'd spin. North Platte, Nebraska, was one of John's favorites. North Platte was home to Buffalo Bill Cody and winter headquarters for his Wild West Show: Injuns, Annie Oakley . . . and John.

"There must have been thirty or forty of those bulls in the ring. Each one meaner than the next! The pony I was riding was green and not used to cutting cattle," the old man explained. "I got in the midst of it and my horse spooked. As he mounted the head of the steer in a panic to escape, the bull's horn caught me in the leg, right there," John stated as he rested his leg on the edge of the table and pointed to his calf. "It ripped the tendon right out. I reached for my saddle bag and grabbed the extra string for my violin."

Joanie looked at her grandpa in disbelief. *This is what Mom was talking about,* she thought, but then she caught sight of his violin hanging on the wall behind him. John was a classically trained musician.

"I spurred that horse over to the side of the corral with my good limb. That cat gut saved my leg!" He winked at Hedvig. "I had the best nurse in the world. Your Grandma stitched me up!"

"John!" Hedvig shouted with a chortle. "Stop filling that child's head with nonsense!"

Later that evening, as Verna tucked Joanie into bed, she asked, "Did Grandpa *really* do all those things he talks about?"

"I've heard these stories all my life," Verna said and added with a shrug, "As you get older, you'll learn to separate legend from lore. In fact, as you get older, you'll have stories of your own to tell."

CHAPTER 29

1954

Rite to Work

Mrs. Dixon's rooster announced the coming of dawn for another day. Joanie pulled the covers to her chin for that last minute of warmth before rising. The guttural chug of the milkman's truck stopped outside the little three-room, cedar-shake house as he made his deliveries on the block.

"Good morning, Bob," Verna said in a whisper as she greeted the milkman at the door. The bottles jiggled and clinked in the wire container as the swap of empties for full was made.

"Joanie! You don't want to be late the first day," Verna called from the kitchen as she switched stations on the radio.

> "Sunny, low sixties; fog burning off by noon. It's a beautiful spring day in the Pacific Northwest. The rhododendrons are in bloom; strawberries ripe for picking . . . so let's take in a deep breath and repeat after me . . . I live where angels vacation," the DJ blathered.
>
> "Speaking of angels, the Blue Angels are going to be at Whidbey Island Air Base this weekend."

"Don't forget your lunch," Joanie's mom reminded her and held the paper sack at arm's length.

"Did you . . ." the young girl asked as she took the bag.

"Yes," Verna responded and held her nose. "I don't know anyone who eats liver sausage and grape jelly sandwiches, except you."

Joanie smiled, grabbed her jacket, gave her mother a peck on the cheek with a cheerful, "Thanks, Mom," and ran for the bus stop.

The cool dampness of the fog kissed her face. Salt air from the sound filled her nostrils. From the bottom of the hill, she could see other school-aged kids waiting for the Strawberry Express. Each age group huddled together at the bus stop, excited about their first day of work. For Joanie and her ten-year-old classmates, this was a rite of passage. You must be ten and finished the fifth grade in order to work in the fields. Pickers were dismissed from school two weeks earlier than other students, a sweet reason to sign up for the season!

From the top of the hill, she saw her mother's silhouette standing in the living room window. *This must be the last memory Daddy has of me and Mom,* she imagined. He left for Japan six years ago and hadn't been back since. Although, he still called Joanie twice a year (right after her birthday and right before Christmas) to say, "Sorry, honey, times are tough." Every year she'd wait for the birthday card that never came and the Christmas present that never arrived.

"Maybe next year," he'd say.

"That's okay, Daddy," she'd tell him and patiently wait for next year.

Patchy fog skirted the valleys in the strawberry fields. The last of it caught on the surrounding fingers of the low-lying hills. The early morning sunlight and gentle breeze quickly pushed the mist aside and revealed red, ripe fruit clusters on the dark green plants.

Hank, a weathered farm worker, pointed his gnarled hand toward the carriers. Each picker took one and climbed onto the open bed truck.

"Get off at the field on the left. They'll show you where to go from there," he said, his voice gruff from too many years of smoking cigarettes.

He took a step toward a couple of teens and yelled, "Don't straddle the rows; you'll damage the crop!" then turned his head and spat a big wad of tobacco juice in the dirt next to the tire of the rusted-out truck. The flatbed, filled with young pickers, bumped and belched its way to the patch, jostling the live cargo perilously close to the edge and the wheels.

Bud, a tanned, affable teenager, handed out the pay tickets as workers lined up. "Pin this 'round your neck and don't lose it," he instructed. "Every time you finish a tray, it'll be punched here," he said, holding the card for all to see. "Turn it in by Thursday, and you'll get paid on Friday. The quicker you pick, the more you'll earn," he bellowed as enthusiastic pickers filed into assigned rows.

"Start at the ends and work to the middle," the field boss said, pointing at Joanie and Carolyn. "Don't overfill the carrier; the berries will roll off and we'll all lose money." He bent over the row next to the girls and popped a handful of berries between his fingers. "Strip the stems before you put 'em in the cartons. Today's crop is going to the cannery."

Straw covered the dirt between the rows of berries. A swirl of the hand exposed an explosion of ripened fruit, some too heavy for stems to support. A twist and a pull on each berry forced it to drop into the empty cartons on the carrier.

"It's quicker picking when the stems are left on," Carolyn told Joanie. This was her second year in the fields, so she should know.

Joanie grabbed a huge berry lying on the ground, but the twist and pop produced nothing more than a palmful of moist mush. She learned quickly that berries too large to support their own weight were most likely rotted on the underside.

Great for throwing, Joanie mused as an impish grin overtook her.

Carolyn saw *that* look and cautioned, "Don't do it! They'll send you home . . . and you can't come back."

Joanie knew her mom was counting on the money she earned to pay for her school clothes. She couldn't let her down.

By noon the kids, sore and stain-saturated, climbed back on the bus and headed for home. A light green discoloration under the quick of the picker's forefinger and thumbnails caused yelps of pain when bumped or touched.

Carolyn reached above their seat to stow her jacket and lunch pail. Her shirt and shorts parted at the waist, exposing the sunburnt crescent mark in the middle of her back. Joanie placed her hand on her waistline and winced from the tenderness she felt in the same place!

"Trade seats with me?" Carolyn asked.

"Sure," Joanie said as she stood up.

"Look at your butt!" Carolyn said as she pointed and laughed.

Joanie knew her pants felt damp but couldn't see the large strawberry stains.

"That one looks like an owl," Carolyn giggled as she poked at her friend's butt.

"Look at your knees!" Joanie retorted.

"I know! By the last row, I crawled on my hands and knees," Carolyn said as she rubbed her legs.

The following morning, groans filtered through the fields as young backs bent to remove more fruit. Pickers moved slowly until the soreness of the first day wore off. By the end of the week, a rhythm emerged and enthusiasm increased, especially on Friday.

The field boss swung the rope on the large bell hanging on the corner of the barn with full force. The gongs echoed through the valley.

"Turn in your crate and pick up your pay!" he hollered into the bullhorn.

Joanie's jacket dragged on the ground as she reached the kitchen door. In the reflection of the door's window, she could see the freckles emerging on the bridge of her nose from a week in the fields. Her pocket bulged with eleven one-dollar bills and change. As she reached for the knob, John opened the door and greeted her with an outstretched hand. She knew his hands were strong, his grip powerful.

He always said, "If you shake someone's hand, don't give them a dead fish. You can tell a lot about the character of a man from the handshake."

Joanie looked up at his steady gaze. She wiped the dirt from her hand on the back of her shorts, took a deep breath, and partially closed her eyes in anticipation of a bone-crunching grip. She cautiously extended her hand to his.

His grasp was warm and firm. She felt a genuine message of congratulations in the exchange.

"Welcome to the family," he said and returned to his workshop.

CHAPTER 30

1957

Ecclesiastes 3

The elaborate brass sign on John's workshop door read: ARTON DESIGN STUDIO. Twelve-year-old Joanie could see him sitting at his workbench as she walked out the kitchen door into the backyard. He was surrounded by rows of fabric and bins of wood, files strewn on the table, renderings pinned to the walls, and a chair prototype mounted on the modeling stand. The smell of metal and sawdust mingled in the air. Floating fibers created a halo around John as he hunched in front of the bare bulb dangling over his workspace.

This was *his* hub of creation, his center of peace in a female-dominated family. He'd pop a handful of finishing tacks into his mouth, touch the magnetic tip of the hammer to his lips, allowing the brad to set, and with one fluid motion, sink each nail with machine precision into the wood. Pfft-tch . . . Pfft-tch . . . Each tool deftly used by a brilliant master craftsman. Pfft-tch . . . Pfft-tch . . .

"Whatcha working on, Grandpa?" Joanie asked as she walked to the end of the old man's workbench, where she could watch and not be in the way. It was taught from an early age that children were to be seen and not heard.

John took a crisp, one-dollar bill from his wallet and placed it in the folds of a letter sitting on his desk.

"It's an expensive proposition, running a country," he said with a shake of his head.

Joanie nodded. She always nodded in agreement with whatever her grandfather had to say, whether she understood it or not.

"The kids running it now are wet behind the ears," John said, feeling compassion for the enormity of the task at hand facing these young men. "They need our help. As Americans, we must do whatever we can to support them."

Joanie continued to nod as John licked the envelope. "This is the greatest country in the world."

"Is that why you're working on this?" Joanie asked as she held a file she spotted on the drawing board. John grabbed at the papers in her hands. Startled, she dropped them, and the two watched the designs and schematics scatter across the floor.

"Sorry, Grandpa," she said as she helped him pick them up.

She slowly handed a drawing to him and asked, "What's an invisible tank?"

The old man looked at her and warned, "This is *not* for your prying eyes!"

She stood motionless as he slipped the file deep within a stack of papers on his desk. "Some things are not to be shared, except with those who need to know."

"Good morning, Dad," Verna said cheerfully as she stood on the studio steps.

"Harumph," John responded. He popped a handful of tacks in his mouth and went back to work.

"Come with me," Verna said to Joanie. "I need your help."

She looked at the girl and wondered what kind of mischief she'd gotten herself into now but said nothing. Joanie gratefully followed her mother back to the house.

Nine-year-old Boola, stiff from age, circled three times before stretching out in the midmorning sun next to the apple tree. Her eyes were always fixed on her young master. When Joanie whistled, the long-legged, short-muzzled cocker obediently followed.

"Clean these out and then fill this one with berries," Verna said as she handed Joanie the two-pound coffee tins.

"Yes, ma'am."

Joanie sat on the back steps, shaking the loose coffee dust out of the containers with a clean cloth.

"Where ya going, Grandpa?" Joanie yelled as he closed the door to the shed with a firm slam.

The padlock slapped against the wall. John spun the tumblers and gave it a tug to make sure it was set. Every week, he made the two-mile trek to town on foot in his brown suit and bowler hat, a manila envelope tucked under his arm.

"I'll be back for lunch," he said with no further explanation.

"What's in the envelope?" Joanie asked.

He looked at her with those steely blue eyes and replied, "None of your business." A corner of the address in European-styled calligraphy was visible under his arm: Washington, D.C.

"What are you up to?" he asked as he tucked the packet closer to his chest.

"Mom wants me to pick blackberries from Sullivan's orchard. Grandma's making a cobbler."

The two of them walked together to the end of the drive in silence. John turned left. Joanie and Boola turned right and dashed down the path towards the orchard.

"Don't fall in the well!" Joanie yelled after the dog as she carefully picked her way through the brambles. The tall grass shimmied as the dog sniffed her way past the apple trees and scrub brush. A startled rabbit bolted from the briars.

Two hours later, the coffee can was three-quarters full, enough for dinner.

"Come on, girl," Joanie called to her ever-present companion.

She bent over to wipe the dirt off her hands on the long grass lining the back wall of the studio. A faint scratching sound came from within. *What's Grandpa doing?* she wondered. She listened for a moment and heard nothing more.

Proudly, she set the canister on the kitchen counter. Verna stared at Joanie's purple-stained fingers and lips, conclusive evidence the tin *could* have been full.

Joanie smiled with angelic innocence as she skipped out the door to her favorite spot in the yard: a rope swing on the apple tree at the end of the vegetable garden.

The young girl loved the smell of fresh earth, felt pride in their organically grown produce.

"Be good to the land, Joanie, and it will be good to you," her Grandpa had instructed her on more than one occasion.

Rural America measures time in seasons, beginning when the ground thaws in early spring until a deep freeze covers the land in winter.

Joanie thought of the cool spring days when the first of the crops were picked: carrots, radishes, scallions, and sweet peas, the latter being Hedvig's favorite. The two sat in the garden, a large pot overflowing with tender pods resting on her grandmother's lap.

Ecclesiastes 3

Hedvig's fingers gently squeezed each shell until it split along the veining with a decisive pop, exposing the row of peas within.

"Two in the pot, one in my mouth," Hedvig said with a smile. "Nothing tastes sweeter than homegrown produce straight from the garden."

Grandpa & Grandma Arton with Joanie

How quickly the calendar pages slipped from spring to autumn, Joanie thought as she looked at the smatters of red, yellow, and orange on the leathered leaves of late summer. Within weeks a bumper crop of apples would be ready for picking. Last year, what they didn't keep, they sold: eighteen bushels in all.

"I'm going to get the mail!" Joanie hollered from outside the screen door. She had sent for a decoder ring yesterday and was positive it would be here today.

"Okay," Hedvig said as she wiped beads of sweat from her face onto the edge of her apron. Steam rose from the pots of water on the stove; the old lady carefully lowered jars of tomatoes into the canner. A ring of bubbles floated to the top of the pot as the boiling water roiled over the jars. After the ten-minute water bath, a familiar POP! proclaimed the successful seal of each jar as it cooled. The pantry burgeoned with a harvest of colorful jars this time of year; sturdy shelves overflowed with green beans, tomatoes, peaches, jellies, and jams.

"Don't wander too far . . ." Verna said as she tightened the lids on a new batch.

Joanie rode her bike to the end of the yard where the neighborhood mailboxes clustered in an uneven line. The garden butted against the row of mismatched receptacles. Potato plants, which stood so lush and green during the summer months, now lay brown and flat on the ground, ready for plucking. The dead tendrils clutched the mailbox posts in withering poses.

Joanie on Bike

"Nobody ever sends me nothing!" the young girl pouted as she slammed the mailbox door and kicked the stones to the side of the street.

"Well if it isn't Chief Rain-in-the-Face," John called after the frustrated girl. "Stick that lip out any further, a bird'll land on it!"

"Daaaaaaad!" Verna shouted as she ran into the garden, carefully avoiding rows of tender shoots from the second planting of cool weather crops.

"Dad! Something's in the studio!" Verna said breathlessly, her arm pointing straighter than a springer spaniel's tail. "It's big. . . . I mean, it's big! Hurry!" she cried.

Ecclesiastes 3

Boola ran between her and the workshop door, barking, frantically. The dog's long ears danced as her front paws lifted off the ground with every bark. Boola charged the studio door, but not one step closer.

John walked cautiously into the shop, a wooden stick in hand. He motioned for the women to wait outside. Wood scraped on wood as he moved farther into the building, pushing furniture and tables out of the way.

Silence . . . Where was he?

Silence . . . Seconds felt like hours.

Silence . . . Then, thud!

The glass in the windows shook. A clatter of metal came from the farthest corner of the shed. Footsteps from John's leather shoes slapped in rapid succession on the plywood floor, marking the unseen course from storage room to workshop to studio. Boola let out a yelp and cowered as John's wiry body cast a shadow over the poor dog. Arms and legs flailing, he cleared the studio steps and frightened creature.

John in garden

"Call the police!" he yelled.

Patrol cars lined the street in front of the house. Cops surrounded the workshop. A command post formed near the apple tree.

"We'll take a wait-and-see approach," the field officer told John.

Neighbors stood at a distance whispering . . . speculating.

"Look at Helen," Hedvig said with scorn in her voice. Verna spun around in time to see her neighbor close her curtain.

Verna's gaze went up the hill. "Sophie's still on the phone," she said with a laugh, "and she just backed away from the window."

An hour passed and then another. The women made coffee and lunch for the officers. And everyone waited. Twilight set in and still . . . no action. Speculation turned to doubt.

"Quiet!" the officer shouted with a motion to the crowd.

The mob hushed.

Out of nowhere, a fine spray shot from the studio door toward the crowd. Women screamed. Men scattered.

An officer crouched behind the apple tree and fired one tear gas canister into the studio.

It was over for the skunk.

Swedish / Scotch / Irish / English Future History

BEGOTTEN: With Love

CHAPTER 31

1958

Forever Changing

Joanie's health and gym class obediently filed up the stairs onto the raised stage in the auditorium and sat in the twenty-six chairs facing the projector screen placed on the short wall. Mrs. Cheney drew the massive velvet curtains hiding the girls from view and with a short blow on the whistle in hand said, "Okay, ladies, settle down!"

The eighth-grade students quickly hushed.

"You're becoming young women," she said as she walked down the narrow aisle. "Soon, you will experience your first menstrual cycle."

Nervous snickers spread through the assembly. The girls covered their ears in anticipation of a blast from the whistle now hanging around the teacher's neck. They weren't disappointed. The shrill sound reverberated in the enclosed space.

Sharon nervously covered her mouth with the back of her hand as Mrs. Cheney reached for the mop bucket in the corner of the stage and placed it on the girl's lap.

A classmate in the front row let out a loud "Tch!" and rolled her eyes. "Everything makes her queasy!" she whispered in Joanie's ear. That comment earned the girls another blast on the whistle up close and personal.

Joanie, her mouth wide open in disbelief, stared at her friend as Linda's lips formed the word *sorry*. The girls covered their ears and stifled another giggle.

The 8mm projector's wheels clacked as the film snaked its way through the sprockets.

"Today you will learn *everything* you need to know about the birds and the bees," Mrs. Cheney said. She signaled for the lights to be dimmed.

Beautiful music and fields of flowers gave way to the graphic: "Your Body."

"Don't get out of your seat," Mrs. Cheney warned Sharon as she saw a silhouetted figure begin to rise.

The class watched intently as a man and woman held hands. Days on a calendar were crossed off. Butterflies flittered and the camera panned toward a white, billowy cloud. As the music swelled to a crescendo, a tiny newborn baby was gently placed in a crib.

"Please exit stage right," Mrs. Cheney said, holding a cool cloth to Sharon's forehead as she wiped the girl's skirt with a handful of paper towels. The dismissal buzzer blared and the students scattered. It was the end of another school day—a week away from the end of the school year.

"Do you really think we see clouds when we have intercourse?" Joanie asked her friend as they walked the five blocks home from school. She felt so mature using *that* word.

"I heard my mom and dad yelling 'Oh, God' when they were in their bedroom," Jeanette responded thoughtfully. "Ya know, Mom *never* says 'Oh, God' unless she's looking at the sky."

"Do you think she saw clouds?"

"I don't know . . . maybe," Jeanette mumbled absentmindedly as she fished in her pocket for a piece of Bazooka Bubble Gum.

Joanie cut across her yard and Jeanette crossed the street, a scene repeated every school day since the family moved to their new house three months ago. They didn't want to move, but the government condemned their land to build a highway. The majestic apple trees were gone. Grandpa's studio . . . torn down. The garden? Asphalt. Neighbors who'd been neighbors for years moved to new homes throughout Anacortes, victims of the same mass exodus on the outskirts of town.

"Life is forever changing," Joanie's mom told her with assurance that everything would be okay, but in the wee morning hours, Joanie awakened to the sounds of her mother's muffled sobs.

"I don't know how we'll pay the mortgage this month," Verna told John and Hedvig as they talked in hushed tones around the kitchen table.

A knot of panic settled in the young girl's heart. She bent over the heat register in the bedroom floor above the kitchen, hoping to hear more.

"You know we'll never go back, John," she heard her grandmother say. "The money we pay in dues for Valhalla will put food on our table right now."

The crackle of the heat exchanger muffled John's response, forcing the teen to press her ear against the grate.

"HE WAS A ONE-EYED, ONE-HORNED, FLYING PURPLE PEOPLE EATER!" blasted through the clock radio with such intensity Joanie lurched forward and scraped her chin on the corner of the metal register. She leapt across the floor and back to her room as quickly and quietly as possible, avoiding the boards that squeaked, heart pounding, face flushed.

"Joanie!"

The teen froze in mid-stride. Did they catch her eavesdropping?

"It's time for school!" her mother hollered at the bottom of the stairwell.

"I'm up!" Joanie yelled back, still rubbing her chin.

"What else can go wrong?" Verna screamed that afternoon as she stood in the pantry doorway. Her arms were filled with jars of spoiled food.

Tears streamed down her face. She easily popped a lid off one of the containers with her fingers . . . and another . . . and another. Juice stained the outside of some jars; mold clung to the inside of others. Green beans, tomatoes, peaches, applesauce: the full winter store—ruined.

"Look at this mess!" she cried.

"Looking is not going to change a thing," Hedvig said as she began washing down the sticky shelves. "Joanie, give us a hand!"

The young girl filled another bucket with soapy water and began to scrub.

Verna's chin quivered as she carried the jars of spoiled food to the compost heap.

"How did this happen?" she asked when she returned and filled her arms with more containers.

"There's nothing wrong with our new electric stove," Hedvig said.

"The jars weren't damaged in the move," Verna added emphatically. "I inspected *everything* before we started canning this past summer."

John slowly walked the length of the storage room adjacent to the kitchen and finally concluded, "This room has no heat."

"What do you mean?" Verna asked as she followed her father.

"This room is a converted porch," John said as he pulled a piece of paneling off the half wall under the jalousie windows. "See? There's no insulation or heat exchange."

"No wonder it was so cold in the kitchen when we had that record frost in September," Hedvig said.

"The change in temperature must have been enough to pop the seals," John concluded.

"What do we do now?" Joanie asked.

"I don't know," Verna said. Resignation edged her words. She hugged her daughter tightly and added, "God will provide. He always does."

CHAPTER 32

1958

Bodings

The hillsides blazed with dazzling autumn color, intensified by the massive stands of dark green cedars. It was a balmy October day. No clue that dreary gray and bone-chilling drizzle would soon cover the Pacific Northwest for months. Dried oak and maple leaves gently floated to the ground and crunched underfoot as Joanie walked the two blocks home from high school.

Her baby face and stick frame made her look younger than her age. This was a curse for any teenager, especially one whose naturally white-blond hair and ivory complexion created no pizzazz. She needed color! Black hair . . . or at least mascara and rouge.

The light pink wool cardigan her mother knitted was draped around her shoulders and offset the rose-colored blouse and pencil-thin gray skirt she wore: hand-me-downs from Ricki St. Andre's lavish closet.

Joanie's hips rolled when she walked just like the older girls.

"You want motion, not commotion!" her friend Carolyn instructed as they practiced their *walks* in Carolyn's backyard before the school year started. Even after three months of application, it took concentration to get that *just right* action.

Janet Nelson's '57 Chevy purred to a crawl beside Joanie. Janet was one of the most popular girls in school and one of the few with her own car. *Why slow down here?* Joanie wondered. After all, she was a junior and Joanie a lowly freshman.

"OOOoooooggaaah!" trumpeted the specialized horn her father had installed on her hot rod. That horn drew kids to the car like a moth to a flame on campus during the week and when Janet and her friends cruised Commercial Avenue with the succession of souped-up cars on the weekend. Janet pulled to a stop next to Joanie.

OMIGOSH, Joanie mouthed while her face was still turned. She swallowed hard and grabbed her purse strap to stop her hand from shaking. Her head felt frozen in space. *Turn your head and smile,* she prompted herself. *For heaven's sake . . ACT CASUAL or she'll think you're an eighth grader!*

"Hey, Joanie!" Janet yelled and waved. The upperclassman's friend, Colleen, was leaning back in the passenger seat. Her feet casually stuck out the rolled-down window and were propped on the side view mirror. Copper pennies in her loafers glistened in the sunlight as did her freshly shaved legs.

"You dropped this," Colleen said as she threw the dirty cardigan in Joanie's direction and said something to Janet that Joanie could not hear. The two of them laughed.

"Sorry," Janet chuckled as she pointed to the cardigan. "I couldn't stop fast enough."

Mortified, the young girl stared at her sweater with the tire tread running up the back and softly muttered, "That's okay."

The car sped down the street with a trailing OOOoooooggaaah hanging in the air. Joanie's self-illusion of *cool* vanished with the car's exhaust.

She hung her head and stared at her oversized saddle shoes (definitely sixth grade) and hairy legs (only in Europe). She felt her embarrassment flush on her face. *Why doesn't Mom know anything about fashion?* Her wants were reasonable: eyelash curler, razor, penny loafers. After all, she wasn't asking for a girdle!

A short leap to the porch stoop, a turn of the knob, and Joanie burst into the kitchen.

"Mom!" No response.

She looked in the walk-in pantry. "Grandma?"

Nothing in there but a trapped honeybee looking for a way out.

"Grandpa!" she called out the back door towards John's new studio. No answer.

This momentous day and she was all alone. Didn't her mother realize how close she came to flunking math? She passed—barely, but passed all the same. Mr. Crow patiently tried to make his points understandable, but Joanie still didn't get the concept of mixing apples and oranges . . . or did he say you can't?

She poured a glass of milk, grabbed a cookie, and sat on the front porch steps. She loved the view of eleven thousand-foot Mount Baker and the Seven Sisters (part of the Cascade Mountains rising from the blue-green waters of Puget Sound). Evergreens dotted the sheer sides of the cliffs like emeralds sewn in the folds of a silver-gray gown. Last October, a forest fire on the eastern side of the range illuminated the rugged peaks with flames and turned the full moon rising, blood red.

Joanie finished her cookie and gasped when she saw her mother struggling as she walked up the gentle incline towards their home. Her empty glass dropped to the ground and rolled down the hill in front of the girl until she kicked it to the curb.

"Why didn't you call a cab, Mom?" Joanie scolded as she rushed to help her staggering mother. Verna squeezed the bags of groceries close to her sides.

"I did, but it never came," Verna said as she sat on the steps of a neighbor's house and waited to catch her breath. Joanie watched her mother's chest heave, her lungs eager for air.

With a deep sigh, Verna slowly rose, picked up a bag, and handed one to Joanie.

"Are you okay, Mom?"

"I'm just a little tired. . . . I'll be fine," she answered with a less-than-comforting smile.

Together, they continued the two-block trek uphill.

"Step on a crack, you'll break your mother's back," Verna recited, taking a wide step over a broken piece of sidewalk. "Grandma will be happy I did that," she bantered.

"Guess what," Joanie asked as the two unpacked groceries.

"What?" Verna responded.

"I passed all my subjects."

"Good for you!" Verna said, beaming with pride. She looked at her daughter and added, "I can't believe you're in high school! I'll never forget your first day in kindergarten."

"Neither will I," Joanie said. "I cried all the way there! Dale Woodruff kept trying to pull up my dress!"

Verna laughed. "It wouldn't have been so bad if you hadn't forgotten your underpants."

"The worst part, Mom, was you marching into my classroom with my undies draped over your arm!"

"You never forgot after that, did you?" her mother said, stifling a grin.

"You did that on purpose?"

Verna flashed an innocent smile, causing Joanie to roll her eyes.

Her mother began to quietly hum, "Doe a deer, a female deer," as she peeled potatoes for dinner.

"Remember when Mrs. Smith tried to teach me how to sing?" Joanie asked.

"She had such a beautiful, soprano voice," Verna recalled.

In falsetto Joanie warbled, "It's not how loud or soft you sing that makes the note sound right, dear. It's up and down." She paused. "I really wasn't mocking her when she asked me to 'Do as I do.'"

"And you figured that out when?"

"When she made me sit in the corner!"

Verna folded the paper bags and squeezed them between the refrigerator and cabinet.

"Do you remember Mrs. Caldwell?" Joanie asked. "She had a reputation for being mean, you know."

"Your second grade teacher? What'd she do?" Verna asked, turning serious.

"She caught me trying to finish my homework in class."

"And?"

"She put her nose to mine and said, 'Have you seen the little girl who used to sit at this desk? I ate her hand! She certainly wasn't using it for penmanship—are you?' Then, she snatched the paper off my desk with those long, skinny fingers and pointy nails. I prayed all year to get through her class with all my body parts!"

"See?" Verna said as she spun Joanie around. "Prayer works!"

BEGOTTEN: With Love

CHAPTER 33

1958

Collateral Offenses

Joanie spent a lot of time in the spare bedroom, dreaming of how she would decorate it once all the boxes were unpacked from the move last spring. Torn pages from the Sears Catalog were taped to the wall, and items she dreamed of buying were marked with bright red stars.

"It doesn't cost a thing to dream," Verna told her daughter. "So dream big!"

The agile teen sat on the floor and used her legs to scoot the heavier cartons to one side of the room. A push too far knocked a paper sack filled with letters to the floor, scattering the contents across the linoleum.

A brightly colored envelope addressed to her mother from her father sat on top of the heap. Joanie opened the card:

> *Merry Christmas!*
> *The baby weighs six pounds, four ounces. Her name is Tomiko.*
> *Tom.*

"What are you doing?" Verna asked as she stood in the doorway.

Joanie jumped and dropped the card. "I was cleaning up and this spilled and . . . I have a sister?" She handed the card to her mother.

"It's true," Verna said, expressing no emotion.

"Why didn't you tell me? Can I meet her? Does she look like me? Can she come live with us? Can I call Carolyn and tell her?"

"You can't tell anyone."

"Why?"

"Because people will talk, and they'll say ugly things."

"Why?"

"Because that's just the way it is."

"Where is she?"

"She was adopted."

"Why?" The surprised girl asked. "She should be with us. We'd love her!"

"I don't think her mother would approve," Verna responded calmly.

The thought never crossed Joanie's mind until that moment. "Daddy had a baby with another lady?"

2Verna said nothing.

"That was wrong!" Joanie screamed. "What's the matter with him? Why would he do that?"

Joanie's face oozed hate. Her fists pounded the floor. "Daddy's done nothing but hurt us!"

"That's not true," Verna said quietly. "If it weren't for him, I wouldn't have you."

"He beat you!" Joanie said with righteous indignation.

"You remember that?"

"I remember all of it! Why did you marry him?"

"Because I loved him."

"Didn't you know he drank?" Joanie asked.

"Not until after we were married."

"Why don't you divorce him?"

"That's not always the answer," Verna said as she wiped the tears from her daughter's cheeks.

Joanie looked deep in her mother's eyes and asked, "What is the answer?"

Verna folded her legs and slowly lowered herself onto the floor next to Joanie. After a long pause, she replied, "Forgiveness."

"How can you forgive Daddy for beating you . . . for beating me?"

"I've not forgotten what he's done!" Verna said as she put the card back in its envelope. "Nobody should stay in a relationship that's violent or degrading. We were fortunate because your father was in the service and shipped out. While he was overseas, he contracted TB and was sent to a hospital in California. I never had to make those hard choices like some families do."

"I'll *never* forgive him!" Joanie said with conviction.

"Yes, you will," her mother replied firmly. "It's hard to forgive someone who's hurt you. Sometimes it feels impossible, especially when the memories are painful. But every night when we say our prayers, we need to ask God to forgive your father."

"Why?"

"Tonight, while you're reciting the Lord's Prayer, listen to what you say: *Forgive us our sins the way we forgive others*. How do you want God to forgive you?"

Joanie took a deep breath and sighed, "Why does Daddy do these awful things?"

"I don't know. I don't think he knows," Verna added. "I do know, when he's sober, he's funny and smart and truly loving, but something happens when he drinks."

"Can't you make him stop?"

"No. I wish I could."

Verna looked at Joanie and said, "All of us make choices in life every day. Some are wise, some aren't. Sometimes, when we want only what we want, it's not easy to remember that our actions affect those around us, as well. When you love somebody and they make poor choices, it's hard to stand by and do nothing. Yet, sometimes . . . it's the most loving thing we do. If we force a situation, we risk losing what we hold dearest. As far as your father goes, I can't change his behavior, and neither can you. Only he can do that."

"Mom," Joanie asked, "do you still love him?"

Verna thought about it for a long time as she looked at the pile of letters and cards haphazardly tossed in a brown paper bag: the meager summary of their marriage.

"Yes," she said quietly. "I just don't respect him."

CHAPTER 34

1958

Out of Order

John arranged the small table next to the bed like a physician prepares for surgery: straight and curved upholstery needles, heavy twine, cotton batting, six yards of ticking, large scissors, and a work lamp.

The heave of padding in the horsehair mattress on which he first bedded his bride sixty some years ago was now depressed five inches lower on her side than his. He planned to tie and tighten the coil springs, smooth the batting, and replace the original blue- and white-striped cover of their bed on this rainy, autumn afternoon.

"Another day of Oregon Mist," Hedvig grumbled as she rubbed her arms for warmth.

"Why do they call it that?" Joanie asked.

"Because Oregon missed it and Washington got it," she explained with a chuckle.

John pushed the window open a crack. The opaque curtain of gray drizzle erased all terrain beyond the neighbor's garage.

"I worked a long time to put those lumps just where I wanted them," Hedvig said to John as she stood in the bedroom doorway. "Now I have to start all over!"

She grabbed the sweater draped over the rocking chair and returned to the kitchen as the timer on the stove chirped. A smell of chocolate filled the house.

A steady patter of rain and the crackle of the metal housing on the oil-burning stove made Joanie grateful to be inside where it was warm and dry.

"Hey, Grandpa," Joanie said as she entered the bedroom. "Mom says it's almost time for dinner." She nervously looked over her shoulder.

"I'm just about finished," he answered louder than usual. And then he whispered, "Did you get it?"

"Yeah . . . what are you up to?" Joanie asked as she passed him a handful of dried lima beans.

"Grandma says she'll miss the lumps in the bed," he said with a grin as he placed the dried lentils between the sheets on her side of the bed. "If Grandma's happy, I'm happy!"

Joanie sat cross-legged on the living room floor after dinner, a skein of yarn held taut between her arms. The fiber pulled ever so gently as her mother wrapped the wool into a ball. Her grandma, legs crossed at the ankle, right over left, mindlessly rocked herself with the heel of her shoe as she crocheted a decorative scarf for the arms of the couch. John played his usual five games of solitaire at the kitchen table with a pack of fifty-two cards worn thin from years of use.

"Joanie, pick a card," he'd say and Joanie would point to one. Without picking it up, he'd tell her what it was. The girl marveled at his psychic abilities. He was always right!

"It's past your bedtime, young lady," Verna announced.

"Can I listen to the radio if the lights are out?" she asked. "Pleeeeeeease???"

"Fifteen minutes . . . that's all! You've got school tomorrow."

"Okay," she sighed and pouted all the way up the stairs. Heavy footsteps on each tread announced to all in the house how she felt about her mother's decision.

Verna called Joanie's name half an hour later. Joanie reluctantly turned the radio off.

"Joanie!" She heard again.

With a deep sigh, Joanie rolled toward the door and cried out, "I turned it off!"

"I need you," was the weak response.

Joanie stomped down the stairs and found her mother on the floor next to her chair. "Mom! What happened?"

"Help me up," Verna slurred from a mouth that drooped on one side. Her arm hung limply in her lap, and her back rested on the seat cushion of her chair where she had collapsed to the floor.

The young girl struggled to pull her mother upright. Verna's limp body was too heavy for the eighty-five-pound girl to move.

"Grandma!" Joanie yelled.

Hedvig ran to the living room, pulling her housecoat around her. One look and she screamed, "John!"

"I'm calling an ambulance," Joanie told her mother.

"Don't," Verna said firmly.

Scared, Joanie followed her instincts instead of her mother's command. She'd never openly defied her mother, but something inside her said she must.

God, don't let anybody be on the party line, she prayed.

"Number please . . ." asked the operator.

"Please call an ambulance. My mother needs help."

———

"I'm here to see Mrs. Elliott," Joanie said to the nurse at the front desk.

"Turn right," the woman in the crisp, white uniform instructed as she pointed south. "Go to the end of the hall. The room's on the left."

Joanie placed her feet on the gray squares of the checkerboard linoleum and tiptoed toward the room for fear the noise from her street shoes would echo in the rooms if she didn't. She saw a tiny figure in the bed closest to the door in the room opposite her mother's. The bed she'd occupied after her tonsillectomy.

"Joanie, is that you?" the old woman called out.

Joanie was shocked to hear this stranger call her by name. Out of curiosity, she entered the room.

"Mrs. Caldwell!" the surprised teen spurted out. "What are you doing here?" Joanie placed her hands behind her back, instinctive after her ordeal in second grade.

"Relax," Mrs. Caldwell laughed. "You made it out of my classroom in one piece; you're safe. What are you doing here?"

"Mom's over there," Joanie said with a nod of her head toward the other room.

"Your mother is very sick," Mrs. Caldwell said as she put her arms around Joanie's shoulders, her voice as gentle as a mother's lullaby. "If you need me, I'm right here."

———

Joanie sat next to her mother's bed, tenderly stroking the stricken woman's wavy hair. She looked so peaceful. There was no response except for one lone tear trailing down her cheek.

Verna was fifty-one years, seven months, twenty-five days old when she died. Her fourteen-year-old daughter was with her when it happened.

Light filtered through the half-windows in the basement of Vera's Chicago home, diffusing the shadows in the unfinished space. The staircase divided the laundry room/workbench area from the location John and Hedvig would call their own until their accommodations at Vikings' Valhalla were ready, sometime after Christmas.

Two sleeper sofas (designed by John forty years ago) formed a conversation pit with Hedvig's prized Persian rug covering the concrete floor between them. An old pump organ belonging to Vera's husband, and badly in need of repair, occupied the far wall.

"Here are the last of your things, John," Vera's husband, Grinnel, said as he dropped a large cardboard box on the floor next to the organ. The sudden impact of the heavy box striking the floor caused a bass note to escape from the instrument in a burst of dust.

John slowly shook his head. "Our whole life summed up in these few boxes," he muttered as he looked around the dank room.

The living room was filled with people. Holiday lights sparkled everywhere. "I never saw so many presents in my life," Joanie said as she picked up a clump of torn wrapping paper and tossed it into an empty box.

"I have one more gift for you," Hedvig said quietly. "It's from us," she added as she glanced toward John. It was a diary . . . complete with lock. The gift Joanie had begged her mother to buy for her.

"Thank you, Grandma," the teen said with a smile before she turned sullen. "I wish Mom was here."

"I do too," Hedvig said. Tears coursed down their faces. The joyful banter of the family gathered to celebrate Christmas clashed with the painful grief entombed in their shattered hearts.

In the quiet of her room, Joanie curled up on her new bed and pulled the covers around her legs. A bitter wind howled and pushed into every crevice with icy drafts of polar air. She opened her new journal to Christmas Day:

>**December 25, 1958** – *Grandma and Grandpa gave me this diary today. I'm only going to write the important stuff. . . starting with November 13th.*
>
>**November 13, 1958** – *Why did Mom have to die??? No child should be without her mother!*
>
>**December 1, 1958** – *We arrived in Chicago. I have my own room and my own bed! It's <u>very</u> cold and windy here. A terrible fire at Our Lady Queen of Angels School killed a lot of kids today. No mom should be without her child! It's not fair, God! I don't mean to criticize, but you shouldn't take people out of order.*
>
>**December 28, 1958** – *Grandma and Grandpa left for Valhalla today. Nobody told me until I came home from school. I never got to say good-bye!*

CHAPTER 35

1959

Best Laid Plans

The phone never rings after 8:30 p.m. unless it's bad news. Vera jolted awake from her sleep on the couch. It wasn't a planned nap, just an evening ritual after a full meal.

"Hello?" she murmured. Her face went pale and her hand trembled as she listened intently. "Thank you," she politely replied. "Please call as soon as you know more."

"What's wrong?" her husband asked, shaking the sleep from his mind. He reached for a handful of chocolate chips in the candy dish on the coffee table.

Vera stared at the floor. "Dad's missing."

"What do you mean he's missing? How can you lose a grown man?"

"He never showed for dinner tonight. Mom said he's been talking about going to Chicago, but she didn't take him seriously."

"Don't they have any security at Valhalla?"

"It's an old people's home," Vera snapped, "not a jail!" Anger smoldered on her face.

"I'm going to bed," she announced and slammed the door to her room.

Andersonville had changed since John and Hedvig lived there sixty-three years past. The magnificent, turn-of-the-century buildings showed signs of neglect. The Scandinavian immigrants who had called this neighborhood home had long ago scattered and assimilated into the fabric of America. Many of the shops were now closed and the streets deserted, except for the occasional college student or entry-level worker who found the cheap rents attractive. Outdated and faded advertising on closed stores hinted at better times.

John glanced at the third-floor apartment window where they raised their family. The "For Rent—Apply Within" sign, although faded from exposure to sunlight, attracted him to the entrance hall.

He tucked the metal file box closer to his chest. It contained a faint and odd odor, not easily identifiable. Not many people would recognize the mixture of tear gas and skunk (a reminder of the standoff in his studio).

"Yes?" The voice on the speaker crackled.

"I've come to rent the room," John answered.

"I don't want any smokers," the voice replied.

"I don't smoke . . . don't drink," he responded.

"I want a month's rent in cash—in advance," the woman said.

"I have it with me."

The heavy, downstairs door latch released with a scrape of metal. "I'm on the third floor," the woman shouted down the stairwell.

Peeled paint chips lay on the carpet runners. The beautiful oak floors were black from years of soot and soil buildup. John slowly walked up the stairs. Verna's three hash marks were still visible on the banister.

Vera defended her big sister back then: "Papa, you mark your tools with three cuts so people know they're yours. We want people to know these are our stairs!"

The ninety-one-year-old man smiled at thoughts of the faded memory.

"It's furnished, you know," the landlady said as she unlocked an outside door to what had been John and Hedvig's bedroom. The inside door to the rest of the house was now sealed. Only an image of the interior entryway marked by cracked drywall tape remained.

"The bathroom's down the hall. No showers after nine p.m. The pipes make a terrible clang," she explained. "Mr. Gorski gets up early."

A bare bulb hung from a cord in the ceiling in the middle of the room. Coffee stains covered the worn folding table and chair nestled under the window. Stored on a rickety shelf an arm's length away were: packets of coffee, tea and sugar, and a battered, two-cup percolator.

John spotted a single cot in the alcove in the far corner of the room with a neatly folded army blanket and dirty pillow (void of case) stacked on the floor underneath. He envisioned the wrought-iron bed with the hand-crocheted bedspread over their horsehair mattress that occupied that same space all those years ago and Hedvig at her dressing table brushing her long, auburn hair.

The only remnant of Victorian beauty in this room was the elaborate crown molding covered with layer upon layer of discolored paint.

"I'll take it," John said and paid her cash.

It had been a long ride into the city and twilight rapidly approached. John entered the all-night diner and slid into a booth.

"I'll have two eggs over easy, bacon warmed . . . not crisp, rye toast, and black coffee," John told the waitress. He handed her the menu. "Lou's got my things in the backroom."

She smiled. "Let me get your order in and I'll get your stuff."

Two men in their early twenties watched John from their booth and talked in hushed tones.

"Thanks, Roxie. Good grub," John said as he picked up the suitcase and shopping bag. He paused on the sidewalk to put his change in his pocket. The streetlamp barely illuminated the coins he held in his hand.

"Let me help you with that, Gramps," the taller of the two strangers from the diner said as they stepped out of the shadows.

John stepped in front of his parcels. "I can do it myself, thank you."

"We don't think you can," the chubbier man chided.

John put his hands in the air and said, "Look, I don't want any trouble."

"Either do we," said the taller kid. His wide smile exposed tobacco-stained teeth.

He lunged at John's left wrist while his partner blindsided the old man with a roundhouse punch to the mouth. The force sent John reeling backward. He fell to the ground on his back and somersaulted to a standing position. He spit blood and teeth.

Both men rushed him. John focused on the chubby attacker. He stepped forward, right hand connecting with a palm slap across the jaw. The thug's head twisted to the left. John delivered a straight-in punch, grabbed the punk's shoulder, and finished him with an elbow strike. The kid let out a scream as the bone in his arm snapped.

The grin left the taller kid's face. He turned on his heel to run as John's shoe wrapped around his ankle. He saw the look of determination on John's face as the old man lay on the sidewalk in front of him. His free foot connected under the knee of the trapped leg. The loud pop of the thief's breaking bone was audible above the man's howl. Both punks lay on the ground, writhing in pain, when the police arrived.

"What happened here?" the officer asked Roxie.

"I called the police when I saw these two trying to rob our customer," she said. "By the time I got out here . . . this is what I saw."

The officer turned towards John. The smiling old man (two front teeth missing) held his thumb in the air and said two words: "Jiu Jitsu."

Hedvig stared out the window, barely noticing the beautifully landscaped grounds at the Vikings' Valhalla home. This was the longest she and John had been apart since they married in February 1904. She sat on her rocker, twiddling her thumbs. Her thoughts paralyzed with worry, her eyes swollen from tears and lack of sleep.

"Morning, Frank," Mike said as he grabbed his hat, baton, and police-issue leather jacket. The shift had just begun. He rubbed the small of his back, his sciatic nerve acting up again. The thought of another twelve-hour shift in the squad car was tortuous, but then the thought of three days off made it tolerable.

"I hear we've got a new BOLO. Who're we looking for?" he asked.

Frank, the young rookie working the desk, slid the sheet in Mike's direction.

"Some old guy. Runaway from the home in Gurnee. He used to live in this precinct maybe forty, fifty, sixty years ago. They think he might be back in the neighborhood."

Mike let out a low wolf whistle as his old partner walked in. "Detective Pearson," he said as he looked his friend up and down, "don't you look sweet! Got a date?"

Pearson showed his fist and said, "Naw. I gotta be in court this morning. My case with the Geiboldt sisters finally went to trial."

He looked over Mike's shoulder and asked, "Who's on the wanted list?"

"Some old guy, a runaway. His family's afraid one of our dirt bags'll rough him up."

"Yeah? What's the description?" Pearson asked.

Mike scanned the report. "His name is John Arton. He's a white male, ninety-one years old, approximately five foot nine to five foot eleven, 185 pounds, light build. Last seen wearing a dark brown suit, white shirt, and bowler hat."

"I know this guy!" Pearson said. "Who's looking for him?"

"It says here the subject must be returned to the Vikings' Valhalla Home in Gurnee, Illinois."

"How do you know him?" Mike asked.

"Some punks tried to rob him last week in front of the diner."

"Is he at Providence?" Mike asked with concern edging his voice. His own father was only a few years younger than John and suffered from the early stages of dementia. He empathized with the family.

"He's not—but the two perps are."

Mike looked surprised.

"He used something he called chu judo . . ." Pearson stammered.

Frank handed an evidence bag to a passing officer. "Jiu Jitsu?" the desk officer interjected with a look of disbelief.

"Yeah!" Pearson concurred.

"The old guy lost a couple of teeth, but he knocked those two punks into next week. What the heck is that, anyway?"

"It's an ancient form of martial arts used by Japanese samurai warriors," Frank said. "My dad's friend taught it to government employees and military personnel all over the world."

"Sounds like that old guy's one tough character!" Mike commented.

"You better take back-up with you when you go pick him up," Pearson said with a laugh as he left for court.

John's can of vegetable soup simmered on the hot plate as he stared at the triangular-shaped, tinfoil cutouts hanging from a wire coat hanger. Some patterns were smoothed over cardboard, some crinkled, all overlapping. He'd touch the hanger with the eraser tip of his pencil and study it for hours. Scribbled notes scattered everywhere.

The knock on the door startled him.

"Who is it?" he called out.

"Officer Mike Vonnegut, Chicago Police Department. I'd like to talk to you, Mr. Arton."

John pulled the plug on the hot plate. His steps creaked on the bare wood floor as he walked across the room and opened the door a crack, the latch still in place.

"Do you mind if I come in?" Mike asked.

"No. Please do," John said, opening the door wide.

"Is this about the two men that tried to rob me?"

"No, sir."

John seemed confused.

"We received a report of a man that fits your description who's missing from the Vikings' Valhalla Home in Gurnee. Do you know anything about that?"

John looked genuinely surprised. "I told my wife I was coming into the city. I have a contract to complete, and I need to be close to my sources."

"Your family's worried about you, Mr. Arton," Mike said. "I can make arrangements to have you transported back to Gurnee."

John shook his head. "This is not a convenient time."

The silver stubble on his face didn't completely cover the fading ribbons of yellow and green from the bruises on his jaw and upper lip. He sat motionless and stared out the window for a long time.

"Am I obligated to return?"

"No," Mike answered. "However, I strongly suggest you contact your family and let them know you're okay."

The officer's eyes took a quick assessment of the dilapidated room.

"I can't force you to go, but I will advise you that I believe it's in your best interest to return."

"Thanks for the advice, but I need to finish what I've started," John said, his eyes darting to the wire hanger.

Mike's gaze followed. "What are you working on?"

"I'm not at liberty to say," John responded as he quickly stuffed the Invisible Tank folder into the metal box.

"When I file my report," Mike said, "I'll note that you've been located but refused to return."

Vera hung up the phone.

"Get the car," she said as she grabbed her coat.

Grinnel's eyes narrowed. "I'm not going anywhere at ten o'clock at night except to bed! I've got to go to work in the morning."

"They found Dad," she said as she held the door open.

"Joanie, let's go!"

CHAPTER 36

1961

Night Visitors

Joanie stood in the middle of the basement, a copy of *Moby-Dick* in hand. Her Hula-Hoop hovered waist high as her fourteen-inch ponytail bobbed with every rotation of the hoop.

"Towards thee I roll, thou all destroying but unconquering whale," she emoted with great stage presence to no one there. She tucked the book under her arm and held the hoop with her fingertips so she could take an illustrious bow for her performance.

She liked doing homework in the dungeon, as she called it. Nobody bothered her. When she sat cross-legged on Grandma's rug and placed her hands around her face to block her side vision, she could imagine being home: Mom's knitting needles clacking as she created a sweater from a ball of yarn; Grandma's rocking chair gliding to and fro; the familiar snap of Grandpa's cards as he shuffled the deck. A momentary delusion in the mind of the sixteen year old that helped her cope with the seemingly unending trauma.

She rested her back on the disintegrating cardboard container filled with miscellaneous items, articles belonging to her grandparents. On top of the heap, a stock certificate from Anderson Manufacturing with a note scribbled on the front in Grandpa's perfectly formed calligraphy: "Easy Come. Easy Go" (whatever that meant). The metal box containing the documents about the Invisible Tank lay on its side in the corner of the carton. Even though more pages filled the folder, she promised not to read it and, as Grandpa taught her, "a promise is a promise."

"Hark . . . thy doorbell ringest," she said to the adoring, invisible audience and bounded up the stairs.

"I'll get it!" she shouted.

Vera and Grinnel barely noticed her slide across the dining room floor with a pirouette into the hallway.

"If it's your friends," her uncle called after her as he looked at his watch, "tell them nine o'clock is too late to visit. And, no, you can't sit on the stoop with them."

Joanie rolled her eyes (not where they could see it) with a "tch" loud enough to pull nails out of wood. She flung the door open.

Three men stood shoulder to shoulder on the other side of the screen. Black fedoras covered their hair; dark sunglasses concealed their faces.

"Get your mother," the man in the middle said gruffly. His raspy voice sent chills through the stunned teenager.

"Achoo!" The shorter man to the right snorted. He pulled his black trench coat back to reach the hanky in his pants pocket and exposed the butt of a gun concealed in a shoulder holster.

Joanie stared, frozen in place. *Get my mother,* she thought. *They have no idea how much I wish I could. I don't think they want to hear she's dead.*

"Can I help you?" Grinnel asked as he pushed Joanie toward the living room.

The men walked into the house and Joanie ran for the kitchen.

"Stay in here," Vera whispered as she followed the scared girl into the kitchen, her aunt obviously shaken by the presence of the night visitors. "And keep that music up," she hissed as she pumped up the volume. Joanie's mouth opened in disbelief.

"Did you say . . . turn it up?"

Vera responded with a nod of her head as she walked back toward the living room.

"La Bamba" rocked the airwaves, and Joanie's stocking feet danced closer to the dining room archway. Not near enough to hear the conversation, but adequately close enough to see Vera and Grinnel turn pale as parchment paper.

The men followed Vera to the basement door located in the short hall leading into the kitchen.

Who are these guys, and what do they want? Joanie wondered as she opened her civics book. She mindlessly flipped pages, hoping to hear something, anything, filter up the stairwell. It seemed an eternity passed before the four returned. The last man, the one with the gun, held Grandpa's metal box under his arm; his head turned to keep from smelling the stench of tear gas and skunk emanating from the container.

"What are you doing with that? That's Grandpa's!" Joanie shouted as she charged for the box.

A powerful grip grabbed her arm.

"Let them go," Grinnel said calmly as he held her back.

"That's Grandpa's papers! He doesn't want strangers looking at them!"

Grinnel tightened his hold on her as the men walked out of the house into the night.

"What just happened?" Joanie asked.

"Nothing!" Vera said sternly. "You saw nothing."

The repetitive sound of the volleyball bouncing on the side of the house echoed through the breezeway. Any other time, the slap of the ball summoned neighborhood kids to the site within minutes, but not today. Joanie walked to the front of the house, stood in the middle of Patterson Avenue, and looked both ways. Nobody in sight.

"Steven!" she called out when she saw the thirteen year old walking toward his house. At the sound of her voice, he began to run.

"Hey . . . Steven, stop!"

He froze in place, nervously looked around, and placed his finger to his mouth. "Shhhhh!"

"What's the matter with you?" Joanie asked.

"I'm not supposed to play with you," he said and backed away.

"What'd you do?" Joanie pressed. Steven was big for his age but shy by nature. She couldn't imagine him in trouble.

"Nothing!"

"Then why?"

"Because my dad says your family's crazy!" the frightened boy blurted out.

"Why would he say that?" Joanie asked, shocked to the core. The dropped volleyball slowly dribbled to the edge of the curb.

"Because the FBI came to our house last night—that's why!"

"What did they want?" Joanie asked in a loud whisper as she stepped closer to the young boy to let a stranger pass them on the sidewalk.

"They wanted to know if we knew anything about the letters your grandpa writes to President Kennedy and the Pentagon!"

"What did your dad tell them?" she asked, knitting the pieces together.

"He said your grandpa's a crazy old coot! He'd have to be to send money to one of the richest men in the world!"

"Stop saying that!" Joanie said through gritted teeth. "Grandpa's not crazy. So don't say that again."

"Or what?" Steven countered, standing nose to nose with the teen.

"That *crazy old coot* knows Jiu Jitsu," Joanie said, flailing her arms over her head, "and he taught it to me!" she said with vibrato, hoping to scare Steven into respect. "Stop calling him crazy or I'll give you a chop!" she yelled, using her body to emphasize the point. She took a quarter turn to the left, her waist poised perpendicular with the ground. With all her force, she flung her right foot straight out. Intense pain shot from her groin to her knee as she overextended her reach. Steven grabbed her arm as she fell into him.

"Sorry . . ." she began to say, but the look on his face reflected total terror. A glance over her shoulder told her why. Steven repeatedly shook his hands from side to side as though that would erase the damage to his father's new car. The driver's door had crumpled like a piece of used tin foil from Joanie's frenzied kick. The two grabbed each other by the shoulders and screamed like a couple of rock-and-roll groupies.

"Omigosh," Joanie whispered.

"Omigosh," Steven mirrored.

"Omigosh," the two cried out in unison as they ran for their respective homes.

Joanie's journal contained ten entries in all from 1958 to 1966:

> ***May 1961*** *– Oh, God, what do I do?* (She wrote about the incident. She never saw Steven again . . . nor his family . . . nor the car.)

> ***November 13, 1959*** *– It's been a year since Mom died. I feel her presence <u>every</u> day. I wish she was here.*

> ***December 1, 1959*** *– Grandma died today. Aunt Vera says it was from a broken heart. Grandpa says nothing . . . he just stares out the window.*

> ***February 26, 1964*** *– Aunt Vera died today of cancer. Grandpa doesn't talk anymore. He's lost both his children and his wife. I sit and hold his hand. I don't know what else to do.*

September 21, 1964 *– We raced to the hospital! Grandpa died five minutes before I arrived. I don't think he should have been alone, but God had other ideas.*

September 2, 1966 *– Daddy found me about a year ago. He lives in Florida now. He called the operator in Chicago and got my phone number. He remembered my married name from the wedding invitation I sent him four years ago, which he never answered.*

I've not seen him since I was four years old, except for one day when I was ten. He's planning to visit next week. I'm twenty-two, married with two children of my own, yet the thought of him visiting makes me feel like a child myself. I don't know what to expect.

September 9, 1966 *– Daddy died today from an accidental overdose of pain pills and alcohol. Four days before our visit. He never could keep a promise!*

In eight years, my whole family is gone.

G-o-n-e . . .

GONE!

CHAPTER 37

2003

At Looooong Last

It's a warm and sunny day—rare for San Francisco, especially along Skyline Drive south of the city. In a matter of miles and minutes, Joanie entered Golden Gate National Cemetery: final repose for thirty thousand military men and women and their spouses. The repetition of white headstones hugged the curvature of the horizon, melting into infinity from the hilltop vista overlooking the bay.

A plane departed and banked on the perimeter of this sanctuary, too far away to break the sound of silence with the roar of its engines. With a seemingly intentional tip of the wings as a final salute, the aircraft disappeared for destinations unknown.

San Francisco's National Cemetery

There's a peace beneath this sod: a fully captured act of contrition and saving grace known only to the dead and our Lord,

God Almighty. All earthly cares abandoned at last breath. The veil of questioning and doubt lifted and full knowledge of eternity now revealed for those who sleep beneath.

For the living, faith in that which cannot be seen nor fully understood filled Joanie with that odd blend of trepidation and hope. Somewhere in this twenty-eight-acre maze of marble and granite monoliths is the grave of her father, Reginald Thomas Weir/Elliott.

The office kiosk issued a map and coordinates. Tom lay buried somewhere within this sea of white. Joanie walked past the graves of service men and women on her search: buffalo soldiers; Civil War veterans; World War I and II heroes; Korean combatants; Vietnam patriots; Iraqi warriors . . . all defenders of American freedom and ideals.

Joanie read and reread the inscription on his stone and placed her hand on the ledger, visible evidence he once lived. Her fingers traced the pitted and faded lettering: name, rank, place of death. A shimmer of white embedded in the stone brought a vision of Chief Petty Officer Elliott standing tall and proud in his dress whites. The row of medals and bars pinned above his heart: Victory Medal II, American Defense, American Theatre, Asiatic-Pacific . . . Good Conduct, pronounced his commitment to his country.

A palpable wash of gratitude swept over Joanie for the courageous pledge her father and his compatriots made to defend our nation. A vow shared by the sacrifices of their families and loved ones.

She sat in hushed surrender and watched the shadows from the grave markers slowly creep across the manicured grass. The awareness that we are all sinners and the knowledge that we all *may* be saved brought her humbly to her knees. One hour passed, then two. No thoughts. No tears. No anger. No hatred.

She closed her eyes and opened her hands in an expression of letting go of all the hurts she'd experienced over the years, real and imagined.

Whatever her expectations . . . whatever her misgivings, when exposed in that brief gesture of forgiveness, vanished on the afternoon breeze. She gently placed a simple act of love from her lips to her fingertips to her father's headstone and strode up the hill into the gathering afternoon fog.

Joanie prepared for take off then settled back in her seat. Emotionally exhausted, she looked forward to napping on the flight home. She peered out the window and watched the ground crew hoist luggage into the belly of the plane.

Her thoughts drifted to her grandmother . . .

> *"Look!" Hedvig yelled as she stood in the middle of the yard. "Joanie, come here!" The little girl ran quickly to her grandmother's side as a large, lumbering prop plane from the Boeing plant near Seattle flew low and slow over their house. "Someday, if you're lucky enough and rich enough, you may be able to ride in an aeroplane!"*

"Excuse me," the stranger said as he stopped, looked at the row number, and glanced toward the partially empty seat. Joanie's blanket and magazine haphazardly dropped where it didn't belong.

"Sorry," she said as she wedged the items between her seat and the fuselage, a common practice of this frequent flyer.

The plane, bound for Chicago, climbed rapidly through the mist. From her window, she spotted a ragged clearing over the cemetery where she'd spent the afternoon. Headstones emerged as thin white lines encircling the American flag. The plane banked gently, and as quickly as the scene appeared, it vanished.

She rested her head against the pillow and closed her eyes. Reality floated through the void of time as sleep overtook her.

It seemed only minutes before the alarm sounded. It felt good to be home and in her own bed. She shook the indistinguishable images of fragmented dreams from her mind and rolled onto her side with a sigh.

Joanie didn't move as quickly at sixty as she did as a teen. She clicked on the television as she did every morning and waited to see what terms the world offered today. No matter what the report, she knew her day would become whatever she made of it. A scribbled entry on her calendar noted: *Country Club Luncheon.*

The television blared from the other side of the room. Her hand searched the top of the nightstand for the remote as her head lay buried under the pillow. The reporter, positioned near the hastily constructed review stand in the middle of a wide-open field, stood shoulder to shoulder with military and political dignitaries. The cameraman slowly zoomed in on an armored tank rolling across the rugged terrain before the newsman spoke.

"What did you think?" the flushed correspondent asked a dignitary about the demonstration.

"If I hadn't been here, I wouldn't have believed it!" the man said and quickly pushed into the crowd to get a closer look.

The reporter turned to the camera and said, "So there you have it. British Defense Researchers unveiled the invisible tank today."

Joanie peeked out from under the covers to look at the image. A belly laugh shook the bed. Her thoughts quickly transgressed

At Looooong Last

from the here and now to her grandfather's studio and the mysterious file that caught the attention of the FBI in 1961.

"You were ahead of your time, Grandpa," she said with a grin.

Somehow, she felt this news flash vindicated an old man and his dreams: a brilliant human being who sacrificed so much and believed to his last breath that his life could make a difference. She turned off the television and headed for the shower. She didn't want to be late.

Joanie waited in the back of the crowded dining room. When she heard her name announced, she took a deep breath, smoothed the lapel on her jacket, said a silent prayer, and walked directly to the podium.

Three hundred beautiful teen faces watched her every move as the audience gave her a warm welcome. These young lives held so much promise; yet, their eyes expressed the scars of emotional and/or physical pain. They stood on the threshold of adulthood, questioning their self-worth . . . even their very right to be. She understood all too well the internal turmoil they faced and how effortless it is to adopt a negative attitude of victim rather than embrace the optimism of survivor.

It had taken Joanie years to understand and accept the traumas she'd endured during her formative years, to learn how to forgive unconditionally and to trust there are happy endings. If by telling her story she could give one person the courage to face their challenges and believe that a brighter tomorrow actually does exist, then the pain she endured had value.

Every one of us has the opportunity to grow in grace and beauty, she thought as she looked into the crowd of young faces. After years of researching her family's roots, she'd come to the conclusion that each generation faced its own trials, celebrated its own triumphs, and stood firm against its own perils. This generation will do the same, and the one after that, and so on.

She remembered all too well not knowing how to heal a shattered spirit. There was a point in time when she wasn't even sure she still had all the pieces. And even if she did, if she could . . . everyone would still see her brokenness.

It wasn't until she learned about the ancient Japanese art form called kintsugi that she began to look at herself and others for the true beauty held within our frailties. Kintsugi is the Japanese word for golden joinery. This technique is used to refurbish damaged ceramics.

According to the Freer Institute at the Smithsonian Museum in Washington, D.C.:

> *Kintsugi is based on the belief that something broken is stronger and more beautiful because of its imperfections, the history attached to it, and its altered state. Instead of hiding what's been damaged, the shards are mended with a special resin mixed with gold dust. The bonded seams become an intrinsic part of the ceramic and add a personalized, one-of-a-kind beauty through its imperfections.*

This is what she saw as she looked into each face: gold . . . pure gold coursing through the delicate porcelain that represented each life before her.

Joanie thanked the Junior League of Manatee County for the beautiful "She's Setting the Pace" award and the opportunity to share her story. Each year the organization recognized someone in the community who overcame obstacles and challenges as a way to motivate and inspire the student body.

"Just like you, I didn't have a choice as to where I was born, the family in which I was raised, the color of my skin, eyes, or hair. I grew up in a three-generational household. We were poor but not impoverished.

"Poverty has nothing to do with social status or financial position," Joanie said. "Some of the richest people I've known had little in the way of worldly possessions, my mother and grandparents included. Poverty is a condition that resides in the heart . . . not the wallet."

Joanie noticed a crowd beginning to form as the wait staff began to line the walls in the back of the hall. She paused and gathered her thoughts. "Unexpected circumstances and decisions made by others—family, employer, government, and God—influenced my life's journey. The same will be true for you. That's just part of life!

"If something changes the course of your dreams, do you give up? On the contrary! Follow your dreams, set your goals, but be receptive. Listen to others. Consider what they say and if necessary, adjust. There's strength and wisdom in life's lessons, and there are adventures along the way that will prepare you to use your gifts in ways you've not yet imagined!

"The most powerful lessons my family taught me, they learned from generations past. It's the message I want to leave with you."

Choose to live with honor and integrity;

In all that you do, be an honest and trustworthy person;

Use your talents to serve others and your country;

Protect and nurture life . . . it's the most precious gift we have;

Develop a personal relationship with God.

Life is filled with challenges. Face them with courage and faith. It's where wisdom and strength dwell.

If you live by these standards, you will never be poor. Your life will be filled with wealth and your heart will truly know peace.

Out of all these choices, the greatest choice we make is to hate or to love.

. . . Choose Love."

— The End —

Acknowledgements

Little did I realize when Aunt Frances handed me the family Bible in 1979 it would lead to this moment! As an only child and a second-generation American, I've longed to know more about my family, to better understand who they were and why these immigrants sacrificed so much for me and future generations. Bill and I met amazing people while seeking answers to those questions. We've walked the towns and countryside of my ancestors and toured homes and workplaces where these families actually lived and died. It's meant years of meandering through cemeteries; searching through newspaper clippings, boxes of faded photographs, and mementos; and viewing thousands of documents (many in foreign languages). This has not been a solitary journey. Many have joined us along the way, and we are forever grateful for their love, support, and super-sleuthing skills.

I don't intend to list all 1,406 relatives we've located, but there are some from the Fisher/Weir and Svensson/Arton clans who deserve a special *thank you* for sharing stories and/or pictures: Frances and "Spike" Elliott, Verna Elliott, John and Hedvig Arton, Lars Eric Ahlin, The Buchholz family (especially Dayna Brock), Chuck and Carol Weir, and Kathy and Jarl Nilsson.

There are many new friends we have made along the way who were willing to share their knowledge and love of history and genealogy when I asked for help. To them we say *thank you*, especially to: AJ and Myrtle Booth for introducing us to Prattville, Alabama; David Mrozinski for the amazing tour of Pratt's Gin Mill and the Fisher family home; Ann Boutwell for offering (a complete stranger) refuge when the hour was late and the distance too great to begin the journey home. Also, *thank you* Ann and Dave for proofing the manuscript to make sure I stayed true to the vision of your town's founding father, Daniel Pratt.

Some of the silent partners in America and Sweden are those working in our libraries, museums, and historical societies. My gratitude to you for helping us find forgotten gems of history, especially the staff at the Autauga Heritage Association; Kathy Jordan from the Grand Junction RR Depot Historical Society; the historians at the Hyde Park Historical Society; Chicago's Museum of Science and Industry, in general; and the main library in Visby, Gotland, Sweden.

A writer's best friends are the professionals who critique, inspire, and mentor during the development process and beyond. This ***thank you*** goes to: Jim Williamson (author of *Lessons Learned* series), whose enthusiasm is contagious and mentoring skills kept me believing in my goals; to Claudia Lowman (Koi Graphics), who planted seeds of confidence; Nancy and Biff Barnes (Stories to Tell), who gently suggested the further development of plot lines; Marilyn Howard (Manatee Community Foundation), who envisioned the finished product with such clarity. ***Thank you*** Police Chief Rick Wells from the Palmetto, Florida, police department and Jim Campbell, a third degree black belt instructor at the Goshi School of Jiu Jitsu in Lakewood Ranch, Florida, for sharing your knowledge in your respective fields. To Marilyn "let's read it one more time" Erfourth (my executive assistant); Erin Roof, a gifted editor and proofreader; Eli Blyden (Crunch Time Graphics) for the amazing cover design; and to my friends from the Retired Educators and Professionals (REAP) Writers' Group who critiqued my completed work and encouraged me to publish.

Thank you to all my friends who have kept me grounded over the years: from Anacortes, Washington, and the Class of '62, from Chicago and Carl Schurz High School (Class of '62), and especially my sisters from Gamma Delta Epsilon. A heartfelt ***thank you*** to my lifelong friends (especially Carolyn Tolentino) and to my amazing husband for his unconditional love.

Most of all, I ***thank God*** for this incredible journey . . . every breath a blessing, every day a gift!

Bibliography

Alcoholism Information, http://alcoholisminformation.org.

Anderson, Goren, (2008). *Bingsby.com*. Retrieved January 2010, from A Medieval Town in Sweden: www.Bingsby.com.

Arton, John, Bed Chair. US Patent 1,336,062, filed September 2, 1916, and issued April 6, 1920.

Arton, John, Convertible Furniture. US Patent 1637797, filed July 26, 1920, and issued August 2, 1927.

Arton, Nils, *Frostasnack i Ringsjobojd* (Lund: Lorentz Larssons Tryckeri, 1942).

Arton, Sven, Sweden Patent 2033604, issued 1937

Arton, Sven, Sweden Patent 130410, issued 1952.

Booth, Myrtle, Misc. Documents, Personal Correspondence, Oral Accounts, 1864 to Current, (Prattville, AL).

Boutwell, Ann, Prattville Geneaology and Oral History, (Prattville, AL).

Brandt, Roger, "Camp Oregon Caves: Stories from the Heart of the Siskiyou Mountains," Archive Report (1934–1940), Oregon History, Cave Junction, OR.

Campbell, Jim (instructor, Lakewood Ranch Taekwondo Academy in Bradenton, FL), private demonstration for the author, 2009.

Canada, Mark, "Antebellum and Civil War America 1784–1865," University of North Carolina at Pembrook, 2001, http://www.uncp.edu/home/canada/work/allam/17841865/.

Centers of Disease Control and Prevention, "*Child Abuse Statistics,*" http://www.cdc.gov/mmwr.

Chefs, P., United States, 1893.

Chick, Drew, "Hundreds of Wildflowers Bloom in Natural Garden Around Crater Lake Park," *Oakland Tribune*, September 8, 1926.

Christian, George,. "The Confederate Cause and Its Defenders.,"*Southern Historical Society Papers,* XXVI, October 4, 1898.

Clark, Josh, "Is the Army Testing an Invisible Tank?" How Stuff Works, October 2007, http://science.howstuffworks.com/invisible-tank.

Columbus Enquirer Weekly Newpaper (1862–1864), Columbus, GA.

Corbett, Edward, *An Old Coachman's Chatter* (London: Richard Bentley and Son, 1890).

Cort, Louise, (curator of Kintsugi exhibit, Smithsonian's Museum of Art), August 2008.

Coulson, William. "Experiences of a CCC Enrollee at Camp Wineglass – 1934," *Crater Lake National Park, Administrative History,* 1986.

Dickerson, E. "Mining Claim Definitions," http://stonegate-realestate.com/resources/claimsInfo.cfm.

Elliott, Archie, Misc. Documents, Family Bible, Personal Correspondence, Oral Accounts, 1911 to Current, (Grand Junction / Ouray, CO).

Fathauer, J. H., "Chicago Notes.". *The Furniture Worker Journal* 37, no. 6 (1920):, 253.

Fedderson, Yvonne, "Child Abuse Statistics," 1959, http://www.childhelp.org.

Ferris, George, United States, Misc. Newspaper Articles, 1893.

Friends of the Viking Ship, http://www.vikingship.us.

Fox, Martin, "President's Report – July 7, 1902." *Iron Moulders' Journal* September 1902: 609–617.

Glim, Jo Ann, Misc. Documents, Family Bible, Personal Correspondence, Oral Accounts, 1890 to Current (Chicago, IL).

Graham, Edward, *R&LHS Railroad and Locomotive Historical Society,* Daly City, CA.

Great Lakes Naval Museum, http://www.history.navy.mil/museums/greatlakes/index.htm.

Harvard University, "Immigration to the United States (1789–1930)" *Harvard University Library,* http://ocp.hul.harvard.edu/immigration/dates.

Heritage Quest Online, http://www.heritagequestonline.com.

Hoong, C., "Crater Lake: 1,000 Feet Below the Rim,". Oregon State University Archives, http://archives.library.oregonstate.edu.

Hoppe, Michelle, "Manners for Women, Part One – As a Single Woman," *Literary Liasons,* http://www.literary-liaisons.com/article031.html.

Hospice International, "Helping Teen-agers Cope with Grief."

Hughes, Robin, (Prattville Heritage Association), in discussion with the author, 2011.

Hyde Park Directory, 1905–1906.

Hyde Park Historical Society, http://www.hydepark.org/parks.

Ives, James, "Colorado Business Directory – Grand Junction – Mesa County," *The Colorado State Business Directory* 37, 1911.

Johnson, Kristen, "A History of the Independent Order of Vikings," *Independent Order of Vikings,* March 2005, http://www.iovikings.org

Jordan, Kathy, (Grand Junction Railroad Depot Historical Society), in discussion with the author, 2010.

Kent, Kelvin, "Bag A Peek / Meek to Eek," *Ouray County Summer Guide,* May 2009, 18–20.

Kubler-Ross, Elizabeth, *On Death and Dying* (London: Routledge, 1969).

Leon, Louis, *Diary of a Tar Heel Confederate Soldier* (Charlotte: Stone Publishing, 1913).

Lewis, Jone J., "Fannie Farmer," *About.com,* .http://womenshistory.about.com/od/cookbooks/p/fannie_farmer.htm.

Lurz, Frank, "Tales of the Bobs," Sharp Shooters Production, http://www.riverviewparkchicago.com/generic17.html.

Mason, Erik, "Was Longmont's John Empson a Robber Baron?" *Longmont Museum,* April 2009, http://www.ci.longmont.co.us/museum.

Mastrogiusepps, Ron, "Prominent Visits, Mrs. Roosevelt Wineglass Camp CCC Boys,". Crater Lake Institute, August 1934, http://www.CraterLakeInstitute.com.

McFeely, William, *Memoirs of General William T. Sherman 1820–1891* (New York: DaCapo Press Inc.,1984).

Melville, Herman, *Moby-Dick* (New York: Harper & Brothers, 1851).

Mrozinski, David, (Continental Eagle Corporation), tour of plant and discussion with the author, 2010.

Mesa County Genealogy Society Library, http:// https://www.museumofwesternco.com.

Museum of Science and Industry, White City Tour (2010), Chicago, http://www.msichicago.org.

National Park Service, "Civilian Conservation Corps," *History Collection RG4*, http://www.nps.gov/hfc/.

Naval History and Heritage Command, http://www.history.navy.mil.

Nepstad, Peter, "1893 World's Fair," *Hyde Park Historical Society*, (2003).

Nepstad, Peter, *Hyde Park Historical Society*, 2003 http://HydeParkHistory.org/Herald.

Nilsson, Jarl, Misc. Documents, Family Bible, Personal Correspondence, Oral Accounts, 1765 to Current, (Sweden).

Nobles, L. (Varied). Oak Hill Cemetery. Prattville, AL, USA: Autauga Genealogicl Society.

*Norway Heritage, "The New World," htttp://www.norwayheritage.com.

Norwegian National League (NNL), "The Viking," http://www.nnleague.org.

Olson, E., "The Swedish Element in Illinois," *Swedish-American Biographical Association*, 1917.

Reiff, Janice (Ed.), "Chicago Historical Museum," *Encyclopedia of Chicago*, (Chicago: University of Chicago Press, 2004).

Reisberg, Barry, "Aging and Dementia Profile/Benchmark System," *NYU School of Medicines*.

"Riverview Park Site," *Sharpshooters Productions*, http://www.riverviewparkchicago.com/homepage.html.

Robinson, Veronica, (Swedish American Museum), personal tour and discussion with the author, 2009.

Rosentreter, Roger "Roosevelt's Tree Army: Michigan's Civilian Conservation Corps," January 2001, http://www.michigan.gov.

S. o. E. Foundation, *Ellis Island*, http://www.history.com/video_Ellis Island.

Schipper, M., "Records of Ante-Bellum Southern Plantations from the Revolution to the Civil War," *Virginia Historical Society* (1995).

Sexton, Joyce, "History of the Fruit Industry in Mesa County," *Western Colorado Research Center – Colorado Agricultural Experiment Station 3168*, September 1910.

South Carolina Department of Archives and History, http://scdah.sc.gov.

Sussman, Marvin and Steinmetz, Suzanne, *Handbook of Marriage and the Family* (New York: Plenum, 1979).

Sundberg, Axel, *Sweden: Its People and Its Industry* (Stockholm: P.A. Norstedt & Soner, 1904).

Tarrant, S., *Hon. Daniel Pratt, A Biography, Eulogies on His Life and Character* (Prattville: Whittet & Shepperson, 1904).

Taylor, Margaretta, "Reconstruction Georgia 101," *Our Georgia History*.

Unknown, "Mining Claims," http://www.1881.com/minedef.htm.

Unknown, "Praises His Wife and Dies," November 27, 1911, (Greeley, CO)..

Web MD, "Small Pox – Symptoms," http://webmd.com.

Weir, Adam, Certificate of Naturalization, May 10, 1893, (Prattville, AL).

Weir, Charles, Misc. Documents, Family Bible, Personal Correspondence, Oral Accounts, 1864 to Current, (Grand Junction, CO).

White, Anna *Youth's Educator for Home and Society* (Chicago: Union Publishing House,1896).

Wikipedia, "United States Presidential Election 1884," http://en.wikipedia.org/wiki/United_States_presidential_election,_1884

*"Adversity does not build character,
it reveals it."*
—Author Unknown

Author's Biography

Jo Ann Glim's professional career (as a disc jockey and copywriter) began in the late 1960s in Chicago on the all-jazz radio station WSDM-FM when she answered a help wanted ad in the *Chicago Tribune* which boldly stated: No experience necessary. The twenty-four year old, whose personal life was in shambles (a six-year marriage on the rocks and no marketable job skills), laughingly thought, *for once, I qualify!*

The Chess brothers of Chess/Checker/Cadet record fame envisioned a station with all-female on-air personalities at a time when only a handful of women were on the radio. This opportunity not only honed Glim's writing and communication skills, but helped establish a market for other women entering the broadcasting field. A highlight for Glim and fellow DJ Jan Bina was a cowritten Flukies Restaurant commercial, which was in contention for a (1969) Clio Award. Through the years, she worked in the following markets: WSDM-FM Chicago (Jazz); KMPX-FM San Francisco (Underground); and KIKI-AM Hawaii (Top 40).

That was the "glamorous" side of her resume—one she is grateful to have enjoyed—but she was also fascinated by the inner workings of business management. Now, remarried and living in the suburbs, she wanted to experience corporate life. Glim began as a file clerk with Kelly Services and throughout the years took advantage of every business class Kelly and the local junior colleges offered. Sixteen years later, Glim retired as an on-site manager at Baxter Healthcare's Human Resources (IV Systems) division . . . still employed through Kelly Services.

The one constant in Glim's life has been writing. As a forty-year veteran of freelance writing, with credits to her name for Hallmark cards and one-liners for nationally known comedians, her credentials also include: a weekly column, "Day to Day Pomposities and Other Illusions," which appeared in fourteen Lakeland Newspapers in northern Illinois for six years and received first-place honors as Best Humorous Column on family life by the Northern Illinois Press Association in the 1980s; and a monthly column, "Spotlight on Non-Profits," for the Manatee County Chamber of Commerce in Florida, which showcased the good works of non-profit organizations in the community and how businesses could help support their efforts.

When Glim decided to write a book, it was intended as a family history (in story form) for her children and grandchildren. It became apparent the story, although personal in nature, shared a universal message for anyone who has profited from the labors and dreams of the immigrant and magnifies the fact that *every* family has its story.

LIKE / Follow on www.facebook.com/JVGlim.author
Blog: www.Only1Way2Write.blogspot.com
Web site: www.BEGOTTENtheBook.com

If you would like to have your copy of *BEGOTTEN: With Love* autographed, order additional copies for groups or events, or are interested in having the author appear as a guest speaker, please email: JGlim@tampabay.rr.com or write Stemma Books, LLC at PO Box 174, Bradenton, FL 34206.

www.ingramcontent.com/pod-product-compliance
Lightning Source LLC
Chambersburg PA
CBHW050626300426
44112CB00012B/1681